MORALITY
EXAMINED
GUIDELINES FOR TEACHERS

MORALITY EXAMINED

GUIDELINES FOR TEACHERS

Lindley J. Stiles & Bruce D. Johnson
Editors
Northwestern University

Chapters by

R. William Barron
Christopher Boehm
Robert Church
Peter Gillan
Bruce D. Johnson
David A. Joseph
Pamela Joseph
John Lee

Susan Dye Lee
B. Claude Mathis
Arthur Melvin
Bryce Nelson
John Nicholas
Joe Park
Susan Stanford
Francis Ulschak

A Publication sponsored by the Center for the Teaching Professions, Northwestern University

PRINCETON BOOK COMPANY, PUBLISHERS
Princeton, New Jersey

Foreword

The chapters for this book provide teachers with a background for understanding the complexity of ethical issues as well as offer specific help for teaching moral values.

The initial question considered, by Joe Park and R. William Barron, is one often debated and concerns whether morality can be taught. The authors, both philosophers, deal directly with the pertinent issues that provoke much controversy among educators over the learning and teaching of value principles. Their conclusions offer little comfort to those who shun responsibilities in this area by claiming either that teaching should be"value free," or else that although morality is learned, it cannot be taught. In Chapter 2, Christopher Boehm, an anthropologist, shows how moral systems evolve as needed cultural guidelines. The extent to which and how multi-cultural moral values may be identified from the variety of prescriptions endorsed by different ethnic, racial, religious, political and social groups are examined in Chapter 3 by Arthur Melvin. His Century III Foundation is a pioneer in conducting workshops across the country to help teachers examine the values they hold and ways to help students to clarify personal values. In Chapter 4, historian Robert Church provides a background of moral education in the schools of the United States that all teachers need in order to appreciate their roles and responsibilities.

How values are learned and, hence, can be taught, is the focus of Chapter 5, written by John Lee, a behavioral scientist, and Susan Dye Lee, a teacher of social studies. Pamela Joseph, a teacher of social studies and language arts, and David Joseph, a psychiatrist, use case studies in Chapter 6 to illustrate how teachers can deal with students who have no value systems at all. Bruce Johnson and Bryce Nelson, teachers of English and history, respectively, examine, in Chapter 7, the values clarification movement, showing both its strengths and weaknesses as a system for teaching values education. In Chapter 8, Pamela Joseph considers the value

v

conflicts teachers currently face in their classrooms and suggests alternative approaches for dealing with them. Francis Ulschak and John Nicholas, experts in organizational development, show in Chapter 9 how transactional analysis may be used by teachers to help students to develop a framework for ethical decisions. The morality of counseling, particularly when practiced by classroom teachers, is considered in Chapter 10 by Susan Stanford and Peter Gillan, both counselors. Finally, in Chapter 11, B. Claude Mathis, a psychologist and pioneer in improving teaching, considers the impact of contrasting theories of learning and teaching in terms of their moral impact. His thesis that teachers should encourage reflective inquiry into moral values, rather than indoctrinary training, illuminates much of the current confusion professionals confront.

Acknowledgements

The writing of this book has had the support of the Center for the Teaching Professions at Northwestern University. By common agreement of the authors and editors, royalties from its sales are assigned to support additional research to improve teaching in schools, colleges and professional schools. The Center, the first of its kind, was established in 1969 by Northwestern University with support from the W. K. Kellogg Foundation of Battle Creek, Michigan. Since its inauguration, the Center has stimulated and supported a variety of research investigations, publications and professional conferences—all aimed at helping professionals to refine their instructional competence, course and curricular content, and faculty participation.

Initially, the Center and the School of Education at Northwestern University sponsored an interdisciplinary seminar concerned with the "Rediscovery of Morality in

Education." Participants included both professors and students. Out of the research and deliberations that the seminar stimulated came the help for teachers this book offers.

Contributors and Consultants

Numerous people in addition to the authors have contributed to the development of this book. Members of the Northwestern Faculty-Student Seminar generated ideas and concepts, helped to refine chapters, and provided valuable criticism of the final manuscript. Out of such cooperative scholarship has come this first book on morality for teachers. A second publication, now in preparation, will deal with the moral issues that surface when theory meets practice in educational institutions. Additionally, the Center for the Teaching Professions at Northwestern University anticipates the publication of occasional papers dealing with vital aspects of education's responsibility for a moral society.

Participants in the Faculty Seminar, other than the authors and editors, included: Charlotte Anderson, Assistant Professor of Education and Coordinator of the Tutorial-Clinical Program of Teacher Education, Northwestern University; Marshall Browdy, Assistant Professor of Medical Education, University of Illinois Medical Center; Donald T. Campbell, Professor of Psychology, Northwestern University; Anthony M. Cresswell, Associate Professor of Education and Management, Northwestern University; David C. Epperson, Professor of Education, Northwestern University; Karen Fox, Assistant Professor of Education, Northwestern University; Pauline Frederick, Graduate Student, Northwestern University; Sieglinde Freed, Student, Northwestern University; Beverly Friend, Assistant Professor of Communications and Humanities, Oakton Cummunity College, and Member of Associate Faculty, Foster McGaw Graduate School, National College of Education; Catherine Goodnetter, Student, Northwestern University; Rev. Charles Lavely, C. S. C., High School Religion Teacher; Margaret Lee, Professor of Education, Northwestern University; Nancy Leonard, Graduate Student, Northwestern University; Ardwin S. Libman, Graduate Student, Northwestern University; Richard A. Podlesnik, Instructor of Psychology and Social Sciences, City Colleges of Chicago; Judy Pollock, Graduate Assistant, Northwestern University; Gustave J. Rath, Professor of Industrial Engineering/Management Sciences, Educational Organizational Development, Director of Design and Development Center, Northwestern University; Victor Rosenblum, Professor of Law and Political Science, Northwestern University; Charles W. Thompson, Associate Professor of Industrial Engineering/Management Science, Northwestern University; Pamela Trent, Assistant Professor of Medical Education, University of Illinois Medical Center; and Roland G. Weiss, Experimental Technological Incentives Program, National Bureau of Standards, Washington, D. C.

The contribution of Michael W. Sedlak to the preparation of Chapter 4 is gratefully acknowledged.

Appreciation is expressed to Dr. B. J. Chandler, Dean of the School of Education, Northwestern University, for his interest and continuing support in this project. The preparation of the manuscript also had help from the following people: Marianne Dahm, Annette H. Dooley, Elena Lonsdorf, Sharon Lee Schultz, and Michael Singer.

The Editors

Contents

Introduction

This book was born of feelings of guilt and frustration about whether education is abandoning one of its historically important responsibilities: the cultivation of morality. On every hand, the authors, as do others, see traditional moral values being disregarded by leaders in all walks of life. It is for this climate of moral malaise, and to teachers and educators who must bear partial responsibility for it, that this book offers help.

The research and deliberations out of which it was developed were carried on at Northwestern University, first in a seminar of faculty and graduate students and subsequently by teams and individual authors working on particular concerns. A common purpose was to reexamine traditional cultural values and to reassess their benefits to society. It was felt that the analyses of moral principles and their teachings are vital to a healthy, self-perpetuating culture. The focus is on teaching because the authors believe that teachers have the ability as well as the responsibility to help shape the moral climate of the future.

Schools and colleges, both public and private, are by tradition and popular demand moral institutions. If they fail to reinforce moral behavior, they will lose the support needed to survive. In return for public confidence, educational institutions are expected to teach students a working knowledge of the moral principles of their society. Teachers, however, do not dictate moral mandates for living; rather, they explain the complex reasons such moral principles have evolved and, in effect, strive to develop a *moral literacy* among students. Thus it is to be expected that when moral decay in society becomes evident, citizens tend to blame schools—and teachers.

Meaning of Morality

Examinations of the schools' responsibility for reinforcing morality quickly become enmeshed in a crossfire of questions about the meaning of morality, whose morality to teach and, even, whether it is moral to teach morality. The authors of this volume generally agree that the concept "moral" refers to the rules governing behavior that have evolved out of accumulated experience essential for group survival. These "moral directives" define conduct in terms of what is *right* or *wrong*. Such rules for living may be written into the laws of a society, but legalization is often unnecessary to force compliance.

Morality connotes conformity to the rules of "right conduct" of an established ethnic, racial, or cultural entity, such as a family, community, bloodline, or religious denomination. Moral behavior is learned. Parents are the prime teachers. Community attitudes and expectations, at least in homogeneous groups, support parental training. Religious institutions offer formal instruction and develop pressures for conformity. Schools are expected to provide additional instruction and reinforcements for morality through the values endorsed, the behavior approved and rewarded, curriculum selections, direct instruction, counseling, and the examples set by teachers and other educational leaders.

Retreat of the Schools and Colleges

In a multi-cultural society such as the United States, differences and contrasting standards of morality make reinforcement difficult, particularly when the agent is a school that must deal with students whose moral commitments vary both in kind and intensity. Inability to identify a common morality for all cultural groups, as well as for all ages, undoubtedly has been a key factor in what appears to be a general retreat of teachers and educational institutions from their role in nurturing morality. Student protests of the late 1960s and early 1970s against conventional moral commitments, in which some teachers joined, have raised additional doubts about professional and institutional obligations to reinforce moral understanding and behaviors. The dream that a "new morality" is emerging has caused other educational leaders to abandon traditional values to make room for their replacements.

Some teachers, of course, have struggled to keep traditional moral commitments. Their efforts often have been carried on against opposition from students, colleagues, and, at times, representatives of the general public. Far too many, unfortunately, have taken pragmatic positions, waiting to see which dominant moral guidelines will emerge out of the current confusion. Others have elected to follow what they hope will be safe, "value-free" procedures, claiming objectivity while refusing to help students to deal with moral issues.

The central purpose of this book is to help teachers to understand the importance of their role in the morality of our society, to know what moral values are and how they are acquired, to suggest techniques for helping students to strengthen basic moral values, and to warn against practices that might be morally harmful or ineffectual. While the book does not attempt to adopt a particular moral position, it is hoped that the reader will be stimulated to think about moral issues in education with a view to taking action to improve the moral climate of the classroom and, ultimately, of society.

Lindley J. Stiles
Bruce D. Johnson

PART 1

MORALITY IN EDUCATION AND SOCIETY

Can Morality be Taught?

Joe Park
R. William Barron

An historic contention of educators is that schools can devolop "moral" human beings. So entrenched is this premise that when breakdowns in moral conduct occur in any segment of American society, teachers are likely to be blamed. Despite the fact that moral accountability is inherent in most educational philosophies, disagreements often prevail about what morality actually is and whether, in fact, it can be taught. Such considerations have philosophic roots that require analysis as well as have practical implications for schools and teaching.

Meaning of Morality

Morality connotes conformity to the rules of "right" conduct. Involved are both social habits as well as responses to perceived necessities of given situations. In a conventional sense, moral behavior is dictated to fit social customs and traditions; more pragmatic perceptions prescribe that adaptations be made to particular situations. When what is "right" in contrasting cultural traditions and adaptations to specific occasions are considered, it readily becomes clear that what it means to be "moral" is not so easy to define. Ernest Hemingway once said, "What is moral is what you feel good after and what is immoral is what you feel bad after."[1] Moral, in this sense, is often used as an equivalent for "right" as contrasted to "wrong," conveying a strong sense of approval or disapproval. "Moral," however, may also be used as an adjective to specify certain distinctions, such as moral problems, moral codes, moral arguments, and moral points of view.

In a narrow sense, morality refers to a particular social behavior. As an illustration, Benny the Dishwasher was alleged to have murdered the three Grimes sisters. The murders were widely discussed in the news media, and there were charges that Benny had sexually molested the girls. The coroner found that this had not occured and issued a statement that, as a consequence, the moral issue could be laid to rest. Sex, in this instance, was a moral matter. Murder, apparently, was not.

Frequently, "morality" may refer to an "instrument of society as a whole for the guidance of individuals and smaller groups." [2] In such instances morality refers to that which "is coordinated with, but different from, art, science, law, convention or religion, although it may be related to them." [3] "Morality" in this sense is a social enterprise into which the individual is inducted, but not exclusively or even necessarily through schooling. This is not to say, however, that most schools do not make morality one of their chief concerns. On the contrary, a school system, by its very nature, reflects the moral and ethical values of its community.

An individual appears to imbibe morality at his mother's breast. His entire life is lived within a moral milieu, and when he dies it survives him. The individual may or may not be particularly mindful of the moral influences to which he responds. As he becomes aware of the moral climate of his times, he may accept it, adjusting his behavior to it, rather thoughtlessly. On the other hand, he may become concerned about its adequacy and take means to modify it. What is significant to note is the individualistic aspect of the social enterprise we have called "morality" and the demand it may make upon reason. Frankena made the point when he wrote, "Morality is a social institution of life, but is one which promotes rational self-guidance or self-determination in its members." [4]

These are the senses in which we shall be using "morality" in this chapter, that is to say, both as a "social enterprise" and as "rational self-guidance." Each consideration of morality involves moral judgments and either societal or self-prescriptions for individual and group behavior.

Moral Judgments

An analysis of what it means to be "moral" involves determining the essential characteristics of morality as well as moral issues. The question of the nature of morality, in philosophic terms, is a weighty one. It can be simplified by thinking of what is involved in a "moral judgment" as it relates to one's actions. The following illustration will help distinguish between a moral judgment and a statement of fact.

Consider the relation between these two statements: "I *ought* to do x" and "I *want* to do x." Is there an important difference between these two assertions and, if so, what is it? Or are moral judgments nothing more or less than expressions of wanting? To begin with, it can hardly be denied that "I want to do x" and "I ought to do x" are both prescriptive. If you state "I want to do x" under normal conditions, then you certainly advocate your own performance of the action x; therefore, the job that this statement performs is that of guiding action, just as in the case of moral judgments. It is, however, important that this similarity between the expressions of wanting and moral judgments not be overemphasized to the extent that the difference between these two distinct types of statements is forgotten.

The crucial difference between expressions of wanting and moral judgments is that in thinking I *want* to do something I am not committed to wanting others to do the same, whereas in thinking I *ought* to do something I am committed to thinking everyone ought to do the same. Thus, moral judgments have the capability of being universalized whereas preferences do not.

Universal Prescriptions

Let us be clear about the notion of universalizability with respect to moral judgments. Consider the following example.[5] Tom, a high school student, has been caught cheating on an exam by his teacher, Dick. Dick, himself, has also recently been caught cheating on an exam by his professor, Jane, in one of his master's degree evening classes. It is the commonly accepted practice in both of these educational institutions for anyone caught cheating to be expelled. Dick admits to himself that he does want to expel Tom. If for Dick there is not question of universalizing his prescriptions then he would obviously assent to the singular prescription, "Let me expel Tom." If, on the contrary, Dick asks himself, "Can I say that I *ought* to expel Tom?" he is faced with whether he is willing to turn his singular prescription of wanting to expel Tom into a universalizable moral judgment. Assuming that Dick is willing to assent to the moral judgment "I ought to expel Tom," it follows that he must accept the universal moral judgment "Anyone who catches someone cheating on an exam ought to expel the person who has been caught cheating."

Being the wise teacher that he is, Dick then realizes that Jane is also in the position with respect to Dick of having caught someone cheating and that if anyone who catches someone cheating on an exam ought to expel this person, then Jane ought to expel Dick. But can Dick accept such a decision by Jane? If he is unwilling to accept his own expulsion, then neither can he assent to the moral judgment "I ought to expel Tom." Only if Dick is himself willing to face the music of his own expulsion can he assent to the moral judgment "I ought to expel Tom." The "moral" that can be drawn from this story is that the principle of universalizability limits moral judgments to those prescriptions from which we do not exempt ourselves or any others.

Perhaps this principle of universalizability sounds vaguely familiar to you. After all, isn't it just another way of stating the Golden Rule: "Do unto others as you would have them do unto you"? If this is the case, then are philosophers such as R. M. Hare guilty of building their own moral commitments into their analysis of morality by means of the principle of universalizability? Hare explicitly pleads his innocence to this charge. He claims, and perhaps rightly so, that although it is easy to confuse them, nonetheless there is a definite distinction between the *logical* thesis of the universalizability principle and the various closely related *moral* theses such as the Golden Rule.[6] According to this point of view, the principle of universalizability is a logical thesis insofar as it is solely concerned with the meaning of moral expressions:

> Offences against the thesis of universalizability are logical, not moral. If a person says "I ought to act in a certain way, but nobody else ought to act in that way in relevantly similar circumstances", then, on my thesis, he is abusing the word "ought"; he is implicitly contradicting himself. But the logical offence here lies in the conjuction of two moral judgments, not in either of them by itself. The thesis of universalizability does not render self-contradictory any single, logically simple, moral judgment, or even moral principle, which is not already self-contradictory without the thesis; all it does is to force people to choose between judgments which cannot both be asserted without contradiction. And so no moral judgment or principle of substance follows from the thesis alone.[7]

The universalizability principle is thus compatible either with the Golden Rule or its denial. It only denies that an individual can hold both the Golden Rule and its denial at the same time without abusing the meaning of moral expression.

As a logical thesis, unlike substantial moral principles such as "One ought to treat others as one would wish them to treat oneself," the universalizability principle does not prescribe any actions. Since neither this principle is equivalent to the Golden Rule nor is the Golden Rule derivable from it, Hare is not guilty of smuggling in a commitment to the Golden Rule within his analysis of morality. The philosophical analysis of morality is neutral with respect to substantial moral principles.

In summary, the philosophical analysis of morality has determined the necessary conditions of moral judgments to be *prescriptivity* and *universalizability*. If a statement is a moral judgment, then it necessarily performs the dual task of guiding action and allowing no exceptions to this guidance. Unlike statements of fact, the moral judgments "One ought to do x" commits one to accepting the imperative "Let me do x, ' and unlike prescriptive expressions of wanting, moral judgments commit one to thinking everyone, including oneself, ought to do x. This analysis of morality as developed by Hare is thus frequently termed universal prescriptivism.

Situational Ethics

If one equates morality with sets of strict "rules" or "principles" for living, a case could be made that conventional morality is outmoded. A foremost proponent of this belief is Joseph Fletcher.[8] His religious version of the attack upon the universalizability of moral judgments is a prime example of what has come to be known as situational ethics of which there are secular as well as religious forms.[9] Situational ethics can be roughly characterized as an attempt to deny the efficacy of any morality that embodies sweeping generalizations that take no account of the extremely complicated character of the situations in which moral issues arise.

Are moral judgments as universal prescriptions such sweeping generalizations? Does universal prescriptivism, either explicitly or implicity, deny the importance of a sensitive consideration of specific situation? If so, we believe Fletcher and the other advocates of situational ethics would not be far from right in claiming that the universal prescriptivist analysis of morality is outmoded. Referring to Hare's work, one can be convinced that universal prescriptivism does not deny the validity of taking specific features of a situation into account in the formation of moral judgments.[10] This defense of universal prescriptivism hinges on the distinction between universality and generality.

Consider the earlier example involving Tom, Dick, and Jane. You will recall that Tom, a high school student, had been caught cheating by Dick, his teacher. Dick had, in turn, been caught cheating in a night school course by his professor, Jane. We insisted that the only way Dick could accept as a moral judgment, "I ought to expel Tom," was to accept the rightness of his own expulsion. As a universalizable moral judgment, Dick's judgment of what should be done about Tom's cheating had to apply with equal force to any other identical situation, even if the judgment prescribed an action to the detriment of Dick, the person who had made the judgment. If, on the other hand, Dick's judgment to expel Tom were singular rather than moral, it would not require Dick to accept his own expulsion as well. Nor would it compel him to accept the expulsion of any student caught cheating at a future date.

Do those who subscribe to situational ethics seriously believe that all moral judgments are singular? Would they have us believe moral education can teach a specific dictum of behavior for any situation? If so, their position seems ridiculous since it reduces moral situations to a series of totally unrelated events. Such belief thereby disallows the possibility of learning from experience. Learning from experience necessarily implies that every new situation is not unique. Perhaps it is not universalizability that the sensible advocate of situational ethics rejects, but rather generality. That is, perhaps it is not the need to apply a judgment to all similar situations that the advocates of situational ethics reject, but rather the advisability of couching a judgment in highly general terms.

Morality, as we have analyzed it, displays two related characteristics. A moral judgment is prescriptive and universal, but these characteristics do not necessitate moral judgments' being sweepingly general in a way that is insensitive to the specifics of the situation. That morality is indeed very much alive implies the importance of moral education. To this end, teachers need not only concern themselves with the training of ethical behavior but must also implant an attitude of moral importance into the subject matter, giving morality a relevant context for all situations.

Is Morality Teachable?

On the surface it seems preposterous to ask such a question. Who could doubt that morality is teachable? We do it all the time, don't we? It may come as a surprise, then, to learn that the question has been debated for a long time.

Socrates, according to Plato, at one time doubted that morality was teachable. In the *Meno*, Socrates argued along these lines. First, the sons of moral men are not moral, at least not in all cases. This is prima facie evidence that virtue cannot be taught, at least not successfully in all instances. Second, virtue can be taught if, and only if, virtue is wisdom and if there are teachers of virtue. But there are neither teachers of virtue, such as there are teachers of mathematics, nor is there a body of knowledge called morality, such as one finds in the conventional disciplines. Therefore, according to Socrates, virtue or morality cannot be taught. How then can we account for virtuous or moral human beings? Socrates' reply was that virtue is "an instinct given by god to the virtuous."[11]   Divine dispensation, however, is not a popular view today, and even Socrates is said to have changed his mind on this matter.[12] What Socrates did not foresee was that there would be deliberate efforts to give systematic instruction in moral development in conventional classroom situations. This instruction often has taken the form of classes in character education, religious instruction and indoctrination, and the imparting of common values and virtues. Again the doubts of Socrates concerning the efficacy of moral instruction appear to have been confirmed. A significant investigation conducted by Hartshorne and May [13] more than forty years ago showed, first, that conventional, systematic, moral instruction in the school setting had little or no effect on moral character. That is to say, character education classes and conventional religious instruction programs apparently had no detectable influence on moral conduct.

Second, deception appeared to have a definite relationship to classroom morale. In some classrooms there was a great deal of cheating, while in other classrooms the level of deceit was much lower. Example and group approval appeared to be dominant factors in the levels of deceit.

Third, some children cheat under many more circumstances than do others. As a rule, these children will not cheat in all circumstances. Perhaps infrequent cheaters are merely more cautious than frequent cheaters.

Fourth, what one knows about desirable behavior does not automatically transfer into desirable behavior. Those who practice deceit are often the most vocal in decrying it. It has been said that prisoners are more aware of Biblical injunctions than are their arresting officers. Moreover, if Watergate has taught us anything, it is that those who engage in deceit and dishonesty express as much, if not more, disapproval of it than those who are less deceitful and dishonest.

Although the findings of Hartshorne and May have not been seriously questioned, different interpretations have been placed upon them. Some have argued, for example, that the moral character of a child is already established before he reaches school. Therefore, the more conventional approaches to moral and religious instruction cannot be expected to have any appreciable effect. Others have been quick and undoubtedly correct in pointing out that many moral character and religious education programs are marked by a failure to exercise intelligence or good judgment. Still others have claimed that morality is composed of emotional tendencies that cannot be adequately measured by conventional verbal tests or contrived behavioral situations. There is undoubtedly some truth in each of these assertions. For example, the effects of the very early years in a child's life are only now being ascertained. Such evidence as we have suggests the supreme importance of these first years.

In spite of the doubts of Socrates and findings such as have been presented here, there are others who believe that moral instruction is possible, if properly conceived.

Kant, in his *Education,* put forth the proposition that morality was teachable.[14] Moral instruction consisted of children learning to act in accordance with "maxims," the reasonableness of which the child must come to see for himself. Ideas as to what is right and what is wrong must be instilled early. It is clear that Kant believed virtue could be taught, but he appears to us now to have been somewhat insensitive to the learner, overly concerned with maxims, and rigid in the enforcement of them. Nevertheless, there is a recognition of aspects of child development in Kant's work that is a forerunner of modern psychology. Kant was not alone in this; Aristotle had recognized that learning was dependent upon maturing of the learner, and the Church has assumed that one could not be held accountable for his sins before the age of reason.

Teaching Morality through Fear

Bruno Bettleheim[15] agrees with Aristotle and Kant, at least in part. He believes that moral instruction is possible provided it is based on fear, conducted in accordance with the reality principle, and regulated in terms of what is known about child development. Bettleheim insists that desirable moral development is impossible unless it is grounded in fear.

Our chief mistake in moral education, he says, is "to believe that what ripe maturity can contain is therefore the best fare for immaturity." The mistake we make is to hope that more and more citizens will have developed a mature morality, one they have critically tested against experience, without first having been subjected as children to a stringent morality based upon fear and trembling. [16] Instead of catering to momentary pleasures and immediate satisfactions, moral instruction should begin in fear, not in fear of hellfire and eternal damnation as in previous generations, but in the more enlightened fears of loss of self respect and love.

Furthermore, for moral education to occur, the reality principle must legislate over the pleasure principle. One might say that a middle class morality exists, the tenets of which hold that in order to gain lasting satisfactions, more immediate pleasures must be foregone. Unfortunately, this is precisely what contemporary education does not do, according to Bettleheim. As a result, children grow up unable to use the educational system unless it is made enjoyable. And, since it is impossible to make all learning enjoyable, children soon become uninterested and turned off. They do not develop disciplined habits of thought so necessary to moral development. Since the vast majority of teachers cannot be inspired and inspiring, any educational system based on the pleasure principle and the assumption that they can be inspired or inspiring must end in failure. As Bettleheim puts it, "if anyone thinks that changing the system will enable us to supply all our slum schools with inspired teachers, then he banks on the millenium instead of planning for reality."[17]

Besides stressing that moral development must originate in fear and be nourished on the reality principle, Bettleheim recognizes that moral development is slow, and appears to follow progressive lines of development. As long as morals were viewed as God-given, immutable, and absolute, it did not much matter that little attention has been given to the nature of moral development in children and youth. Morality could be conceived as essentially the same for young children and adults. Now we seem to be learning that this is not the case. The moral development in children significantly differs from that in adults. This fact is important for those who hold a very conventional view of moral education. It is equally important for those who wish to educate children as if they had the capacities and inclinations of relatively more mature adults. The conventional moral training may provide little or no place for reflective moral decision making. On the other hand, to indulge in complete freedom to choose relative morality and the pleasure principle before developing a stable moral base (in fear?) from which to work may make genuine reflective morality impossible in adulthood.

Developing Individual Integrity

It should be made clear that Bettleheim's views are not universally accepted. For example, Rogers[18] is utterly opposed to Bettleheim's contention that morality must arise out of fear. He suggests that the natural moral choices of children are to be trusted, and that our moral confusion and doubts arise out of injected values that are accepted in childhood because of the threat of loss of love. Once accepted, morals are difficult, perhaps impossible, to examine objectively. One need not, however, feel forced into making the kind of either-or choice suggested by the conflicting theories of Bettleheim and Rogers. One can take a middle ground, such as that of Kurt Baier who advocates a kind of moral education or moral reasoning similar to legal reasoning.[19]

As tempting as it is to indulge in further remarks on Bettleheim, Rogers, and Baier, it may be beneficial to turn to psychologist Lawrence Kohlberg who, unlike Bettleheim, has undertaken a systematic cross-cultural study of moral development in children. Kohlberg[20] holds, with Hartshorne and May, that while moral acts are largely determined by situational factors, they are also related to two general aspects of child development. These aspects are what Kohlberg calls "ego strength" and "levels of development of the child's moral judgments." As he once wrote:

> The first general aspect of the child's development is often termed ego strength and represents a set of inter-related ego abilities, including the intellectual prediction of consequences, the tendency to choose the greater remote reward over the lesser immediate reward, the ability to maintain stable, focused attention, and a number of other traits. 21

But Kohlberg suggests that while "ego-strength" (sometimes referred to as "will") has something to do with moral action, it does not take us to the core of morality or to the definition of virtue. The core, he believes, is to be reached through research in the structure of moral development.

Following the lead of Jean Piaget, Kohlberg has built a "typological scheme describing general structures and forms of moral thought." This typology was constructed after nearly twenty years of careful research, some of it cross-cultural. The typology is based upon a study of the moral thinking of children. It avoids, therefore, the errors of research based upon what adults *believe* to be the nature of moral thinking in children. Moreover, the research is an improvement on Piaget's work in that Kohlberg used a larger sample, a standardized interviewing procedure, and appears to be more conscious of bias on the part of judges. The moral situations he used in his studies are, however, noticeably skewed in the direction of legality versus welfare and justice. Moreover, "moral thinking" is not equivalent to "moral acts" done in the heat of a genuine situation. What one thinks he would do is not necessarily that which he would in fact do.

Kohlberg's typology contains three levels of moral thinking. Each is comprised of two related stages. The levels and stages are considered separate moral philosophies, or distinct views of the socio-moral world through which children pass in order to grow up.

The moral levels and stages may be summarized as follows:

(1) *Preconventional Level*

Stage one is marked by orientation toward punishment and respect for superior.

Stage two is characterized by a pragmatic "scratch my back" morality.

(2) *Conventional Level*

In stage one, the person is concerned with conforming to the majority, and often judges behavior by the intentions of the actor.

In stage two, the concern shifts toward authority, fixed rules, and social order.

(3) *Postconventional Level*

In stage one a "social-contract" mentality and an emphasis upon the possibility for legal changes in the context of rational consideration dominates.

In stage two, the orientation is in the direction of self-chosen moral principles, logical comprehensiveness, universality, and consistency. Human dignity becomes a genuine concern.

There are, we believe, several conclusions that Kohlberg has reached that are pertinent to our discussion.

First, as we have seen, moral thought, like cognitive development, may progress through stages. While a person may become stuck at any level or at any stage, his moral development possibly will be sequential and it will not skip a step.

Second, the levels of moral thinking appear to be independent of any particular religion. Kohlberg found no important differences in the development of moral thinking among Catholics, Protestants, Jews, Buddhists, Moslems, and atheists. On the other hand, class differences are noticeable. Middle class children are more advanced in moral thinking than working class children.

Third, children and adolescents grasp all stages up to the one they are in at the time. Never, however, do they comprehend more than one stage beyond the one they are in. But, more importantly, "they prefer the next stage."

Fourth, a person who understands justice, for example, helps create a moral climate in which justice can be realized. As a result, Kohlberg has remarked, "the universal society is the beneficiary."

Fifth, a person who has not thought through his moral convictions cannot be said to *possess* moral convictions." Instead he has unquestioningly accepted somebody else's standards to govern his actions. His actions may reflect an immediate concern for his own self-interest (prudence) but hardly a commitment to act in terms of logically comprehensive, universal, and consistent moral principles in which human dignity is a genuine concern. To promote this kind of morality is to seek the highest level of moral thought we know.

In sum, although many of the more conventional models of moral instruction have proven ineffective, there is a substantial body of opinion that supports the contention that moral instruction is possible. Now if morality is teachable, how shall we go about it?

Considerations for Teaching

As we address ourselves to the question of how to teach morality, there are, first of all, three general matters for consideration. These serve as background to the more particular ones.

First, it may seem trivial to spend much time making this distinction, but it is a fundamental one. If "moralizing" refers to judgment concerning individual principles, values and behaviors are thought to be proper or improper in a given situation; and, if "moral education" refers to the task of instilling a point of view, but more than that in preparing students to maintain a self-reliance within this point of view, then a fundamental distinction for education has been made.

Moral education is not "preaching" or "strict discipline," or "indoctrination"; rather, it has a rational component, as Russell, Hare, Frankena, and Dewey have argued. It is disciplined thinking. Reasons are appropriate to moral education, and some reasons can be shown to be more appropriate and persuasive than others.

Israel Scheffler summarized it well:

> If moral conduct is our goal in moral education, we are, in effect, striving to achieve not alone the acquisition of norms of a given sort in practice, but the reflective support of norms of this sort in an 'objective' and 'impartial' manner. It cannot, on the other hand, be denied that a serious attempt to accomplish this second (reflective support) may delay and even impede the achievement of the first (acquisition of norms). (To encourage a *reflective and impartial* critique of norms may lead to a rejection of our norms). [22]

Thus, moral teaching, whether in school or outside of school, resembles instruction rather than indoctrination. That is to say, instruction is marked by an openness, while indoctrination is characterized by closedness. The indoctrinator is looking for signs of trouble such as disinclination to accept as truth that which is being advocated. Quests for evidence are shied away from or ignored. Instruction is the reverse of indoctrination. The evidential condition is paramount, and conformity to the belief of the instructor is secondary to the ability of the learner to continue his quest for what is true or what may be the moral thing to do.

Role of Theory

Second, there are difficulties encountered in justifying moral principles and moral decisions. Ethical statements are neither amenable to proof, as are mathematical propositions, nor subject to demonstration as are scientific propositions. Every decision in the moral realm appears to rest upon some moral premise that in turn rests on still another moral premise. If one opposes, for example, the blocking of highways by truckers who are protesting the cutback in fuel supplies and the reduction of speed limits, one may support the position by citing the fact that the delivery of food and mail will be delayed. The truckers may declare that their blockage is justified by their loss of money due to the increased cost of fuel. But equally basic to the argument is an appeal to some moral premise such as, "One ought not to inconvenience others solely for economic reasons," or "My rights come first."

Third, any course of moral action, or any program of moral education, rests upon some theory of justification. That theory may be rooted in the theology many people learn in their youth, or it may be based upon a denial of a distinction between the moral and natural sphere. G. E. Moore claimed it may be established on an intuitive substructure.[23] Perhaps it rests upon a pessimism bred of the contemporary predicament. That is to say, there appears to be no way out of a paradoxical and hopeless contemporary world situation made worse by the fact that our moral decisions can never be demonstrated true or false. This latter theory of justification, if it can be called that, is more prevalent than generally supposed, and has done inestimable harm in that it is responsible for the retreat from reason that is now so widespread. Some theoretical structure, though, is to be found lurking behind the scene in any course of moral action or in any program of moral instruction. Often its presence is unknown to the person or persons involved.

We submit that these are not insignificant considerations, and they are helpful in our search for leads as to proper modes of instruction. But they are not particularly helpful with respect to procedures for instructing.

Research on Moral Instruction

In addition to the insights that educational theory can contribute, it is important to consider the contributions of the science of education. Has research turned up any useful clues?

Kohlberg and Whitten [24] have summarized research on moral instruction. They found that not a very great deal can be said with certainty, except that: (1) Post-conventional teachers and mothers are better moral educators than conventional mothers, (2) Moral development (in Kohlberg's terms) is fostered when parents and teachers listen carefully to the child's moral judgments, rather than demanding conformity. This, apparently, is a confirmation of our earlier point: indoctrination is incompatible with continued moral development. A recent study of legal practices at the nation's five military academies affirms this conviction. It is said to show that "an alleged disdain for legal technicalities, such as lack of sufficient evidence is combined with an exaggerated sense of honor and integrity to produce an attitude of moral superiority." This in turn enables the nation's highest-ranking officers, eighty-five percent of whom in the Army and Navy are academy graduates, "to accept a My Lai massacre or fourteen months of secret bombing of Cambodia as protection of the nation." [25] (3) It is worse to work from too low a level, than from too high a level. In other words, err on the side of a higher level. To communicate at a level lower than the child's stage is to invite a loss of respect. (4) If you wish a sense of justice or honesty in your classroom or home, create an atmosphere of justice and honesty. This is the 'hidden curriculum." (5) A person who comes to understand and accept a moral principle as his own and who has had experience in applying it, will be more likely to abide by it. Thus, moral instruction should be thorough, and it should provide for practice in life situations. This, however, is one of the weakest points in our chain of moral instruction. Materials to promote the discussion of issues are becoming rather sophisticated. [26] But the courage and insight to connect specific normative issues, arising in a community setting, to moral instruction is lacking. [27] And this is a form of moral education in itself. In the process we teach as if our young were to avoid live and controversial moral issues. This, of course, is impossible, for controversial issues are all about us and the decision to deal or not to deal with moral issues is itself controversial and moral.

[1]Ernest Hemingway, *Death in the Afternoon* (New York: Charles Scribner's Sons, 1932), p. 4.

[2]William K. Frankena, *Ethics* (Englewood Cliffs, N. J.: Prentice-Hall, Inc., 1963), pp. 5—6.

[3]Ibid., p. 5.

[4]Ibid., p. 6.

[5]R. M. Hare, *Freedom and Reason* (Oxford: Clarendon Press, 1963), p. 171.

[6]Ibid., pp. 30, 31.

[7]Ibid., p. 32.

[8]Joseph Fletcher, *Situation Ethics: The New Morality* (Philadelphia: The Westminster Press, 1966), p. 26.

[9]Actually, utilitarianism is the term philosophers usually use to depict the secular equilvalent of situational ethics.

[10]Ibid., pp. 38, 39.

[11]Benjamin Jowett, tr., *The Dialogues of Plato*, vol. 1 (New York: Random House, 1920), *Meno*, p. 380.

[12]Ibid., *Protagoras*, pp. 81—130.

[13]H. Hartshorne, Mark A. May, et al., *Studies in the Nature of Character* 3 vols. (New York: Macmillan Company, 1928—30).

[14]Immanuel Kant, *Education* (Ann Arbor, Michigan: University of Michigan Press, 1960), pp. 83—121.

[15]Nancy F. Sizer and R. Theodore Sizer, "Moral Education," *Moral Education*, (Cambridge, Mass: Harvard University Press, 1973), p. 140.

[16]Ibid., p. 87.

[17]Ibid., p. 93.

[18]Carl Rogers, *Freedom to Learn* (Columbus, Ohio: Charles E. Merrill, 1969).

[19]Kurt Baier, "Moral Autonomy as an Aim of Moral Education", ed. Glen Langford and D. M. O'Connor, *New Essays in the Philosopy of Education* (London: Routledge & Kegan Paul, 1973), pp. 96—114.

[20]Lawrence Kohlberg, "The Child as a Moral Philosopher," *Psychology Today* (September 1968): 25—30. Kolberg has summarized his research in several places. See, for example, "A Cognitive-Developmental Approach to Moral Education," *The Humanist* (November—December 1972): 13—16.
Kohlberg is by no means the only person to have completed research of this kind. R. F. Peck and R. J. Havighurst, *The Psychology of Character Development* (New York: Wiley, 1960), postulate five moral character types that are conceived as successive stages of development. Jean Piaget, *The Moral Development of the Child* (London: Routledge & Kegan Paul, 1932), was among the first to conduct such investigations. See Norman Williams and Sheila Williams, *The Moral Development of Children* (London: Macmillan Education Ltd., 1970), for a general introduction to the psychology of moral development, and also Norman J. Bull, *Moral Education* (Beverly Hills, Calif.: Sage Publications, 1969).

[21]*The Encyclopedia of Education*, vol. 6, s. v. "Psychological View of Moral Education" (New York: Macmillan and the Free Press, 1971), p. 400.

[22]Israel Scheffler, *The Language of Education* (Springfield, Ill.: Charles C. Thomas, 1960), p. 95.

[23]G. E. Moore, *Principia Ethica* (Cambridge: Cambridge University Press, 1959).

[24]Lawrence Kohlberg and Phillip Whitten, "Understanding the Hidden Curriculum," *Learning* (December, 1972): pp. 10—14.

[25]*The New York Times,* December 16, 1973, p. 46.

[26]Alan Lockwood et al., *Moral Reasoning: The Value of Life* (Middletown, Conn.: Xerox Corp.), 1972. This unit of instruction in the social studies is built around Kohlberg's ideas. *The Humanist's Manifesto II* could be used as a point of departure for such instruction. See also John A. Zahorik and Dale L. Brubacher, *Toward More Humanistic Instruction* (Dubuque, Iowa: William C. Brown Company, 1972).

[27]Hartshorne and May, *op.cit.*, p. 453, wrote as follows on this point.
> (1)　What is to be learned must be experienced.
> (2)　What is to be experienced must be represented in the situations to which children are exposed.
> (3)　If what is to be learned is some form of conduct or mode of adjustment, then the situations to which children are exposed must be opportunities to pursue interests that lead to the conduct to be learned.
> (4)　This conduct must be carried on in relation to the particular situations to which it is the preferred mode of response.
> (5)　A common and potent factor in such situations is the established practice and code of the group, which by coloring the situation may either hinder or assist the acquisition of desirable responses on the part of its members.
> (6)　If standards and ideals, whether already in the possession of the group or not, are to function as controlling factors, they must become a part of the situation to which the child responds and assist in the achievement of satisfactory modes of adjustment to those aspects of the situation which are independent of these standards and ideals—they must be tools rather than objects of esthetic appreciation.
> (7)　The achievement of specific standards, attitudes, and modes of conduct does not imply their integration. Integration is itself a specific achievement.

2

The Moral System

Christopher Boehm

We all know intuitively what morality is and we all know, more or less, how to operate within such a system in making every day decisions concerning what we should do or avoid doing; yet there exists at present no comprehensive framework for thinking about this important domain. In this chapter an overview is presented of morality that permits all dimensions of the moral system to be taken into account.

Defining The Moral System

Essentially, a moral system is a major component in a total socio-cultural system. Its basic function is to keep individual behavior "harmonized" to the degree that the society in question can function with reasonable efficiency.

Every system of morality includes moral values—ideal ones and also the real ones by which people actually operate. These values work in concert with various sanctioning mechanisms that control individual behavior. The values guide the way, while the various sanctions press individuals to follow a delineated path.

Morality may be defined in numerous ways, and many approaches are possible when trying to find explanations for how moralities work. A number of formal academic subfields are devoted to morality, for example that part of clinical psychological theory that relates to the development and operation of the superego, or that part of sociology that deals with social control. A few developmental psychologists, notably Jean Piaget and Lawrence Kohlberg, have proposed sequences with qualitative differences that accompany stages of morality in the life cycle, and Roger Brown, a social psychologist, has written the definitive work on the acquisition of morality. [1]

In addition, philosophers traditionally have dealt with morality. Their discussions, however, tend to be technical and narrowly focused on trying to clarify a few key definitions. Theologians discuss ethical issues, but usually do so without drawing back to consider the nature of an entire morality system. For a period of time, anthropologists were interested in the investigation of exotic cultures in terms of whether they were shame or guilt-oriented. Findings of such studies were largely inconclusive. In general, anthropological field investigations necessarily have involved some descriptive study of morality simply because these studies were holistic, and morality is a universal and important aspect of culture.

Characteristic of all of these treatments of morality is a piecemeal attack upon just a few aspects of a more complex social phenomenon. This chapter offers a more systematic approach to the description or discussion of moralities, in a framework that allows us to take into consideration the intricate nature of morality systems as they actually operate in everyday life. Such a vantage point is important if we are to consider morality in a context as complex as education.

Morality may be defined in various ways. The contrast discussed in Chapter 1 between "want" and "ought" is one; anything that carries the idea of "ought" or "should" is moral. The idea here is of prescription: a person *should* do this or that. Morality includes *proscription* as well: there are things one *should not* do. Intuitively, or from religious and family training, we all know fairly well what these things are as we operate in our own immediate milieus, although we must often deal with confusing ambiguities.

When we look across cultural boundaries at the values other people live by, it is not always easy to identify moral values as opposed to other kinds. For example, the Navajo Indians consider the accumulation of a substantial but not excessive amount of wealth to be a moral duty; for others, such commitments are considered to be only economic values. Similarly, the boundary between esthetic and moral values can be quite ambiguous from one culture to the next. How, then, are we to identify a values domain that deals only with morality, and in a way that does justice to the culture we are trying to understand—be it our own or a more exotic one?

If values in general are concepts of the undesirable and the desirable, we may say specifically that moral values are those that relate to desirable or undesirable conduct, motives, and attitudes of human beings interacting with other human beings. Since moral systems also involve sanctions in addition to values, we may define more specifically the domain of morality as existing wherever such values are involved with mechanisms that control individual behavior. Most such controls are social and include not only "primitive" legal systems and the kinds of formal legal systems found in complex societies, but also indirect controls such as gossip, ridicule, ostracism, and other kinds of direct group pressure. In the case of children, parental control, which may be direct or indirect, is exercised.

While active physical punishment sometimes figures in moral control systems, many other kinds of social control exist. In addition, individuals may have strong control systems built into their own personalities in the form of conscience or something similar that produces moral discomfort when the moral code is violated. Anticipation of guilt can be an important deterrent, especially in a society where a great deal of anonymity is available to potential wrongdoers. Aside from guilt, moral feelings, and concepts that are widespread across different human societies, there are obligation,

honor, and shame. These are important in the operation of a
moral system, for it is by focusing on the avoidance of either
shame, loss of honor, or guilt that the individual tries to live a
reasonably moral life.

How does all of this add up to a system? The knowledge
of what is right and wrong, combined with the various social
and psychological controls outlined above, as interpreted by
individuals in their own thoughts and feelings, and as
reflected in their behavior, is what constitutes a morality
system.

Morality and Cultural Diversity

If we want to ask why we have a moral system, one
answer is because human beings could not live together without it. To paraphrase the anthropologist Clyde Kluckhohn:
human life is moral precisely because it is social.

More recently, Donald T. Campbell, the psychologist, has
emphasized morality from a new perspective, i. e., its place in
the evolution of culture. [2] According to him, traditional
morality has served not only to suppress disruptive behavior
of individuals, but has lent a beneficial continuity to the cultural life of all human groups.

But the definition of what is right and wrong may differ
greatly from one culture to another. This is exemplified by
the variety of ways in which different cultures deal with the
problem of homicide.   Among the Greenland Eskimos,
traditionally a man who killed another person was only
lightly censured and was given mainly additional respect.[3]
There was no formal sanctioning mechanism for punishing
such people, although what we know about the Eskimo
personality indicates that Eskimos are brought up to have a
great deal of control over their emotions. [4] Some other
Eskimo groups handle this differently. They have blood revenge by kinsmen of the slain person.

In a more fully developed vendetta system, homicide is
not normally directly punished in any way. The community
stands aside.   But every such homicide triggers a feud or

series of retaliatory killings that has formal mechanisms for its pacification once the parties to the feud are willing to accept intervention. At that point it commonly happens that all the deaths and wounds are counted up and the party that is ahead makes a blood payment to even the score. In such negotiations, no account is taken of who started the feud, or of the righteousness of the original killing.

As can be seen, many people in the world have managed to deal with homicide without the benefit of centralized political authority backed up by police power. This does not mean that they do not have a morality system or a sense of morality concerning homicide. In fact, in most such societies there are special cases of homicide that are viewed as "murder," that is, an act that the community both morally condemns and punishes. But in those cases where blood feud is called for, the killings that occur in the course of the feud belong not to the *ought* but to what people *want* to do: they are a normal fact of life and do not have intrinsically negative moral implications, as long as the rules of feuding are followed. Interestingly enough, blood feud indirectly does make for social harmony in that its presence is a strong deterrent to homicide. People think twice before starting a feud that will bring disruption and grief to their own clans.

Most often feuds involve whole kin groups or clans, and any male member of one may kill any male of the other and still be following the rules. This may seem barbarous in the sense that we tend to look down upon such "savage" customs, but on a much larger scale we ourselves have done the same thing in warfare: there, one person may kill another so long as it is in accordance with international law; this form of killing is set aside as not morally reprehensible so far as individual homicide is concerned.

Different Kinds of Moral Codes

Moral codes consisting of what we call norms, standards, or values are to be found in every culture. In certain of their structural features and a few important items of content they

are universal. For example, in every culture there is an ideal
moral code consisting of a series of behavioral propositions
about how things ought morally to be. The *ideal values* that
are represented in our Bill of Rights and in the Ten Commandments are good examples because realistically we know
we cannot hope to fully live up to all of them. Interestingly,
nonliterate cultures also have ideal values, as do members of
urban street gangs. While there are many disparities from one
culture to another, certain threads do hold constant. Honesty within the group is always valued, insofar as it is impossible for a society to operate without trust, and theft must be
limited, as well as excessive greed and indiscriminate
lust.

While we may have difficulty in even beginning to live up
to an ideal moral code, we are saved from this strain by the
existence of a second (also universal) kind of moral code
consisting of *real values*. Real values contrast with ideal
values in that they are not involved in lip service to the idea
of a perfect moral life based upon higher principles that an
average individual may scarcely hope to fulfill. Many
Americans, for example, have been taught to feel in a basic
way that it is never wholly correct from the moral standpoint
to tell a lie. Yet we have the vitally useful category "white
lie" by which we actually operate. Strictly speaking, the
ideal code is in conflict with the real code here, but most of
the time we feel it little because we are used to operating by
our real values. In a way, real values may be seen as rules for
breaking rules.

It is important that real values be clearly distinguished
from behavior itself. If ideal values tell us never to lie, and
real values condone not only white lies but lies to enemies,
we nevertheless *may* tell a lie to a dear friend for personal
advantage and so violate both the ideal and the real moral
codes simultaneously.

After reading this discussion the reader might well ask
why do we have ideal values at all? The recent Watergate
catharsis provides an excellent answer. In every society there

is a certain degree of hiatus that exists (and is tolerated by most people) between ideal values and real values. In the author's view of the Watergate affair, the American public finally became morally distraught over the too great distance they perceived between the Nixon Administration's real values and the higher, ideal values of the United States Constitution. Although at the beginning of Watergate the actual behavior of the government officials involved was viewed widely by most as somewhat immoral, many Americans felt that this was not all that unexpectable in government. But as the public came to realize the extent of the gap between the actual operating values of government officials and the real values held by Americans at large, moral indignation grew. It focused on the President himself and on the fact that he lied repeatedly in a situation in which a "moral" man would have acknowledged his mistakes. The result was the destruction of trust. It is noteworthy that once this disagreement concerning the level appropriate for real values came to a head, ideal values, rather than real values, were cited as a rationalization for unseating those in power. Ideal values from both the Ten Commandments and the United States Constitution came into play. (It is of course, in the school that the ideal values in the Constitution and Bill of Rights are learned through formal teaching. And it is also in the school where many other kinds of ideal values—and real values as well- are learned.) Ideal values in this instance provided a rallying point to focus upon when cathartic moral reform was in order.

Moral Ambiguity and Moral Behavior

Earlier, the moral system was characterized as having the *basic* function of controlling individual impulses so that social life is possible. Here, we look at what may be called *superficial* aspects of morality, examining contexts in which individuals must make choices in the face of moral ambiguity, or choose to manipulate the basic moral system for their own expedient purposes.

Americans, like people of other cultures, tend to operate
under real and ideal value codes often without being conscious of the discrepancy. As we shall see later, for most
people a moral values position is usually highly sensitive to
context, and either or both of these codes may come into
play depending upon the exigencies of the situation.

One result is that we generally think of the ideal code
when we want to talk about the subject of morality, whereas
in everyday life we actually operate more in terms of the real
code. This leads to contradictions. Even though "Thou shalt
not steal" is recognized as an "ideal" rule, many young
people in America view certain forms of "ripping off" as
morally legitimate or even morally desirable. In fact, a fair
number of their teachers probably share this attitude to some
extent—at least when they prepare their income tax.

With a little reflection almost anyone can think of behavioral areas in which he or she regularly goes against ideal
values without really feeling a moral transgression is involved.
In other cases, one is torn between the two. In addition,
most of us may at times simply disobey both kinds of rules,
real and ideal, and do something that we know perfectly well
is wrong. In other, more ambiguous, cases, we may find ourselves rationalizing to make things come out so that we feel
"moral" in terms of reasonable, real standards, if not by ideal
ones.

Cheating in the classroom is an example we all know well.
Most students have found themselves torn between the ideal
code and the often multiple real codes that prevail within the
peer group. Individual differences are also a factor. One
student may feel free to cheat wantonly when the teacher or
the mode of teaching do not inspire respect. Another may
cheat freely in any context at all. Another may never cheat
without feeling extreme guilt. Thus, while the ambiguities in
the moral system are part of a fairly consistant cultural pattern, there are many different ways that an individual may
relate to these patterns.

Teachers who try to enforce the "no cheating" code may encounter moral difficulties. On the one hand, they may wish to reinforce the ideal values they believe in. On the other hand, it may violate an equally moral sense of fair play to make an example of the unfortunate person who gets caught when almost everyone is cheating. A teacher in such a situation is in a dilemma because there really are two different cultures—that of most students, and that of the teacher. The teacher's method of dealing with the problem will itself constitute a form of moral teaching, either through the moral arguments employed or simply through the example offered for emulation or rejection.

The law is another good area for exemplification. A legal code is an ideal moral system in that it contains ideal values spelled out in negative behavioral terms. The discrepancy between ideal and real values is well exemplified in cases of archaic laws that are left on the books but never enforced, or in laws that are not taken literally as written, as is true at present of many states' drug laws with respect to marijuana possession for personal consumption. On the other hand, the ideal code may be used as an instrument of reform, as in New York State where a mandatory heavy sentence for drug offenses was implemented with the intention that it be applied literally. In this case it was intended to do away with the discrepancy between ideal and real values by building in a mandatory twenty-year sentence with no possibility of parole.

In complex societies, the working of the formal legal system of course does not result in an impartial administration of justice, since wealth purchases the most effective lawyers, and juries and judges are sometimes prejudiced strongly in one way or another. This situation itself is a focus for moral concern, since our ideal values predicate absolute fairness whereas most people's real values seem to demand only the absence of truly scandalous inequality. The result is that the judicial system as a social control is subject to considerable variability and even manipulation.

The reader will see that moral codes are by their very nature fairly ambiguous. The fact that we usually are able to operate within this ill-defined framework, not only easily but unconsciously, makes it unnecessary for us to think much about the moral system for everyday living. But in this book our purpose is to scrutinize our moral system and the many ways in which it is involved in education. To do so, it is beneficial to examine and understand as much as possible of the system within which we operate.

The Separate Moralities of Children and Adults

Early in life, children are subject to parental rules and manipulation or punishment. This is where morality is first encountered. How it is learned and what its developmental stages are like is the subject matter of Chapter 5.

If the child first encounters the moral system through the mediation of parents, the peer group is widely recognized as a second crucial factor. Here, the subtler forms of moral learning and social control come into play. We have yet to recognize adequately the need to view the culture of our own children as an exotic culture fully as worthy of serious anthropological investigation as that of Bedouin herdsmen or nomadic hunters and gatherers. It is in the peer group that much vital moral development occurs, and this begins in the street, in day care centers and kindergartens, and of course in school.

We know some of the forms of pressure that arise in groups, often in a moral context so far as the children are concerned (although we might not agree with the values they express or imply). Young children can be cruel in their use of ridicule or ostracism, and of course physical retaliation or attack is another mode of social control. The entire pre-occupation with popularity, while only partially moral, suggests a kind of tribal system where high public esteem is a goal that influences all behavior.

In adolescence, American processes of growing up involve considerable rejection of societal or parental values. But it is a mistake to view such responses as necessary periods of "confusion" or phases when moral values are lacking. Indeed, the culture of children at different levels of maturity contains variants of the American moral code that, while different and in some ways contrary to the traditional code, are nevertheless quite coherent and internally consistent.

Lincoln Keiser's book *The Vice Lords*, for example, portrays the life of a Detroit street gang that consistently devotes itself to a heroic style of life based on interpersonal and intergroup physical combat. [5] For the Vice Lords, this lifestyle is morally desirable.

A Fact of Life: Morality is Complex

By this time the picture of a moral system is taking shape. We have described a concatenation of values and controls that can be called a system of morality, but there are in fact a number of such sub-systems, stratified by age group or stage of development. In addition, we live in a society of diverse ethnicities, religions, social classes and subcultures that necessarily have contrasting moral codes. The differences may be easy to spot at the ideal values level. But real values are usually somewhat harder for teachers to identify, especially when complicated by the additional differences between children's culture and adults' culture.

To make things more complicated, in a complex society such as ours, not only is there a multiplicity of moral codes in operation, as mentioned earlier, but there are individual differences as well within given groups. Where enough individuals in a particular group, or in the country at large, come to *share* a variant value position, a basis exists for conflict or change. The so-called sexual revolution is a case in point.

The proliferation of bases for differences in moral values in modern complex societies has resulted in an overall moral system that is polymorphous both in its values content and in some of its controls. These values and controls must either compete or coexist. While this choice appears to be quite

intricate theoretically, we deal with it fairly well in everyday
life because as members of American culture we all share
some major features of morality, regardless of the sub-group
to which we belong. One reason we may not think about it
more is that so much of our behavior in this sphere is unconscious and therefore unexamined. The effort to integrate
what is known about morality into a systematic approach is
intended to spur us to think about what it is that we are
doing by providing a coherent framework for moral intro-
spection.

Morality and Ethnic Diversity

Another reason we do not deal with the moral complexity before us more effectively is that specific information is
lacking.   We do not have, for example, adequate cultural
descriptions or ethnographies of the morality systems of
seven-year-old Chinese-American children, or of fifteen-year-
old members of the "drug culture." Such descriptions will
come as anthropologists turn their interests toward the study
of education and American ethnicities, and begin to focus
more on research topics that promise to provide information
that is needed for practical application.

In a classroom situation, knowledge of moral cultural
facts may often be crucial when teachers try to help motivate
students whose backgrounds provide them with built-in disadvantages. Especially at first, moral rationalizations for the
acquisition of formal academic knowledge may have to be
quite different for different kinds of children. For example,
the heroic morality system of street gang culture often
creates a block to learning in a situation motivated by middle
class moral values that stress individual development for a
"normal" American life.   Usually, good academic performance is moralistically disapproved of in the heroic culture
of the street.

Obviously, a teacher who does not understand the child's
goals and moral outlook and the kinds of moral controls the

child is used to responding to may have a very difficult time devising a successful strategy for helping to motivate the child work productively. This is especially so if the child detects a note of moral superiority or disapproval towards the culture or social class he or she represents. As teachers, we may emanate such attitudes without realizing we do so.

How the System of Morality Works

If the overall function of the moral system is to provide the necessary modicum of order so that a society may survive in terms of its own internal needs and also compete successfully with other societies, it is also true that moral systems adapt to change and sometimes even may be responsible for very large changes themselves. In terms of cultural evolution, variability of course is the stuff of which new adaptations are made.

Perhaps the most amazing thing about the morality system in America is that it is complex and uncontrolled. Except for formal legal control and police authority, the American moral system operates largely according to its own dynamics, with a highly variegated conscious input from the clergy that generally tends to reinforce ideal values. According to Campbell, there is also an unconscious and unexamined bias on the part of clinical and other psychologists in the direction of getting rid of the repressive aspects of the morality system in an effort to become free of tradition.[6] He suggests that in the name of individual "freedom" we may well be trying to throw away a useful societal tool (namely, tradition) that has been refined by millions of years of cultural and biological evolution.

The Place of the Teacher in the Morality System

Moral systems come in many categories: national, ethnic, regional, and right on down to the individual home or the classroom, which is a kind of mini-system of morality possessing most of the features of the larger systems. Regardless of the diverse moralities present in a classroom, the teacher to a certain extent creates a specific moral universe within that room that functions as a moral system in the sense it has been defined here. Thus, the very mode of control used in the classroom is a form of teaching morality.

Intuitively, a teacher may make practical use of this little moral system, for example by meting out group punishments that focus the moral indignation of the group on a culprit who is otherwise difficult to handle. In another situation, delivering a sermon on having better behavior in the classroom may prey effectively on guilt feelings, and so on. This is done unconsciously, for the most part. We have little precise idea as to which aspects of such practices are liable to affect the children, and how strongly or permanently. It is a whole process that needs to be studied.

In addition, the school curriculum contains a great deal of morally valuative material. This is discussed thoroughly in Chapters 6, 7, and 8, but deserves mention here because it places the school squarely in the arena of the moral system. The values of the teacher, too, sometimes unobtrusively give a moral tone of one sort or another to the facts.

This leaves the teacher alone in a classroom creating a small moral world in which young people will learn morality directly through values (ideal and real) that are taught as subject matter, more indirectly through responses to moral controls exerted by the teacher, and through indirect cues. This is an important world as far as the moral system as a whole is concerned. All adults can recognize within themselves moral values learned in the first or second grade.

An assumption of this book is that the school and the classroom have a very important role to play in American morality. Another is that the involvement of morality in the formal content of classroom teaching is inevitable. Since this is so, it is important that we begin to reflect upon what we have been doing in the past. We must also consider whether in the future we wish to learn enough concerning morality and education so that we may evaluate unconscious policies and face the issue of whether we should begin to tamper with this important educational aspect of the moral system.

[1] Roger Brown, *Social Psychology* (New York: The Free Press, 1965).

[2] Donald T. Campbell, "On the Conflicts Between Biological and Social Evolution and Between Psychology and Moral Tradition," *American Psychologist* 30: 12 (December, 1975): 1103—26.

[3] Jeannette Mirsky, "The Eskimo of Greenland," in *Cooperation and Competition among Primitive Peoples*, Margaret Mead, ed. (Boston: Beacon Press, 1937), p. 70.

[4] Jean L. Briggs, *Never in Anger: Portrait of an Eskimo Family* (Cambridge, Mass.: Harvard University Press, 1970).

[5] R. Lincoln Keiser, *The Vice Lords* (New York: Holt, Rinehart and Winston, 1969).

[6] Campbell, *op. cit.*, p. 1123.

3

Cross-Cultural Moral Values

Arthur I. Melvin

Secondary moral values are culturally based, as suggested in Chapter 2. Primary guidelines for group life, such as the need to control aggression or to protect and nurture the young, have biological roots that are common to all primates, including human beings. As human beings socialized and became dependent upon each other, the necessity for accuracy and honesty in communications became a universal need for survival. Similarly, other premises about human relations, i. e., the maintenance and fulfillment of life, the need for love and security, and the need for accountability, have emerged as necessities for all human beings.

As civilizations advance, individual cultures, economic classes, and ethnic and religious groups, as well as political systems, flourish—often in competition with each other. To ensure the survival of such subgroups, each evolves its own value systen to define the "rights" and "wrongs" of human interactions. These culture-based "rules for living," or moral values, often serve to discourage rather than promote cross-cultural cooperation. Other byproducts of such parochialism in moral values—in early as well as in contemporary times—have resulted in conflicts that have spawned a variety of reform and revolutionary movements.

In view of the cultural value mandates that have often divided rather than united people, there is an urgent need to analyze and to understand the value perspectives that have universal or cross-cultural validity.

Conflicting and Changing Moral Mandates

Where homogeneity prevails in a country or a community, cultural mandates are taken for granted since everyone has been taught the same rules for living. With the increased mobility of people throughout the world, and particularly within an industrial and urbanized nation such as the United States, "cultural purity" in a social sense is more myth than reality. As a result contrasting moral systems are increasingly competing for acceptance. Differences in moral standards found among the various racial, ethnic, religious and political traditions come into sharp focus in the schools, which are expected to reinforce the teachings of parents and community codes for moral behavior. Under such conditions, teachers are confronted with choices regarding whose values to reinforce. Even when predominant home and community values seem to provide adequate guidelines for instructional emphasis, questions persist in the minds of professional educators about whether minority moral traditions are being properly respected.

Morality, like the weather, may seem to be forever changing. This truism holds even in monolithic cultural groups when considered over a sufficient amount of time. What was held to be "wrong" for one generation of a racial or religious group may appear to become "right" for the next, or vice versa. Such change is characteristic, particularly of secondary values, which tend to generate less from popular endorsement than from fundamental social needs. It may affect, however, more primary moral guidelines, such as those related to sexual behavior or control of aggression. In current times, traditional values in the United States are being challenged and disregarded. Many people have become bewildered and disillusioned to the point where they are questioning the basic moral premises on which society and its institutions were founded. The impact on children and young people, particularly, is profound. Daniel Yankelovich examined the moral commitments of 3,000 youths, through interviews, lasting from one to two hours each, conducted in 1967 and again in 1973. His conclusions were:

> Startling and permanent changes in values have occurred in the nation's youth . . . deepening general decline in respect for traditional sources of authority . . . [Referred to are] sweeping changes in sexual morality, work-related values, mistrust of our basic institutions and other challenges to traditional beliefs and values.[1]

The response of schools and teachers to the moral conflict and confusion that prevails has often been more ostrich-like than professional. Condemned, and at times dismissed, for teaching or not teaching, or for teaching the wrong moral values, teachers have tended to turn their backs on such responsibilities. A convenient cop-out has been the myth that formal education can and should be value free. Another rationalization (considered in Chapter 1) has been the claim that morality cannot be taught. Perhaps the most powerful evasion of all has been the assumption (examined in Chapter 7) that value choices are merely personal preferences and unrelated to moral commitments. A more defensible explanation for the abdication of responsibilities for teaching moral values in schools has been the frustrating realization that inasmuch as behavior is learned, initially at least, more by imitation than through rational analysis, teachers cannot hope to counteract by their own examples and organized instruction the immoral models children and youth experience daily through the mass media and, too frequently, in the behavior of some of their own parents, peers, and neighbors.

If teachers and schools are to exert their moral influence, it seems clear that common agreements must be reached about the basic moral values that are essential for the social survival of all. Such cross-cultural agreements, once they are analyzed and understood, can function as guidelines not only for instruction in homes and the schools but also for behavior of members of the sub-cultures that compose communities and nations. Most importantly, cross-cultural moral values can serve as guidelines for evaluating moral influences on the lives of children, young people, and adults.

Moral Valuing: A Universal Process

Our inability to agree about the basic meaning of moral valuing as a process is a key cause of much of the prevailing confusion. The literature on this subject reveals an abundance of semantic disagreements as well as considerable inconsistency in logic. Distinguished scholars, as well as amateurs, take part in this controversy. Baier and Rescher observe:

> It is no exaggeration to say that we do not have available even a suitable terminology in which to record . . . values and we are still in a worse position with regard to determining the soundness of values. [2]

Most discussion of moral values assumes the existence of behavioral responses that are prescribed by a social group or endorsed by an individual. Those compatible with the needs of the group and/or the individual are considered good while others are viewed as bad or evil. Hence, the term moral connotes conformity to socially approved behavior of a group to which one belongs. If a person feels no strong identification with the moral guidelines of a group but wants to be a moral person anyway, behavior is usually guided by a personal set of principles that govern one's relationships with others.

A problem with such cultural group and individual approaches to moral values may be their incongruity with reality. Both assume a set of rules to be followed and both consider a value to be a constant condition—something to which one attests allegiance—rather than a rationally analyzed and consciously accepted choice. The concept of moral value, in fact, is treated as a fixed and unchanging mandate, prescribed by some authoritative source such as science, a political leader, one's self, or one's idea of deity. It is evident that if each group or individual is convinced that a specific choice of words to describe the rules for living are the best and the only ones worthy of endorsement, respect for and understanding of the value choices of others will be limited.

Valuing, in contrast, is a personal process of making choices rather than accepting the decisions of others. Its goal is to discover through an analytical process the primary premises about human relationships that have universal applications. In such an analysis, one confronts the choice of "what ought to be done" in terms of recognized universal ethical principles, rather than "what is preferred" for some personal temporary satisfaction. Out of such valuing can come understandings of the moral commitments of individuals from differing, religious, political, economic, intellectual, and social groups.

Approaches to Valuing

Some of the various approaches to determining values, or to valuing, are more concerned with and offer more promise for the identification of cross-cultural values than others, as the brief descriptions of the predominant approaches below illustrate.

Traditional Authoritarian Approach

Historically, the traditional approach to defining moral standards has been authoritarian. A religious organization, a political system, an ethnic or racial group, or schools may prescribe standards of behavior in terms of what is right or wrong, as judged by a Supreme Being or someone in power who presumably has special wisdom. The specific value mandates or prohibitions often dictate the only acceptable value perspective. The ultimate implication is that everyone should adopt and live up to the prescriptions.

Little latitude exists in many authoritarian approaches for defining cross-cultural moral values, since dogma often limits tolerance for differing traditions. Often rules cannot be applied to fit realistic life conditions.

The rigidity of this approach plus the external imposition tends to violate the sensitivities of those who believe they should think for themselves in order to be accountable for their actions. Throughout history, such absolutism in moral standards has served to provoke individual rebellion and outright renunciation. Recently, some have advocated a new form of authoritarianism as a source of moral prescriptions. For instance, Jacques Monod, the French molecular biologist who won the Nobel Prize in 1965 for discovering the replication mechanism of genetic materials, calls for the development of an elite to set up arbitrary absolute values to insure control of the world. [3]

Cultural Relativism

Another approach to imposing moral values, with authoritarian roots, holds that all behavior must be directly related to the ideals, goals and requirements of the culture. Conformity and positive adjustment to the mores and rules of the cultural or political group are compelled by systems of rewards and punishments. Values are defined by the conditions existing within the culture. Indoctrination, modeling, coercion, peer pressures, and counseling are some of the procedures used to force compliance. Little opportunity exists for rational inquiry into the reasons for moral mandates; people are expected to accept the prescriptions as a condition of membership in the group.

Situation Ethics

A move away from authoritarian and culture-oriented impositions of moral requirements is the approach that argues for moral decisions to be made by individuals in terms of each specific situation. In some cases, the valuing may be done by a group and imposed on members, as in the case of a nation's decreeing that aggressive killing in war is morally justified. Similarly, a government may impose stringent standards for individual behavior during times of crisis because the situation requires such conformity. In short, situation ethics has long been an instrument of politicians, militarists, and unscrupulous leaders in any area who seek to justify digressions from traditional moral standards.

In recent years, the philosophy of situation ethics as a personal prerogative has been gaining momentum. [4] Individuals argue that they should decide what is right action in terms of the conditions confronted. Thus, if one is hungry, stealing can be justified. If a government is corrupt, or makes mistakes, disloyalty and rebellion are seen as justified reactions. In personal applications, too frequently, it comes down to the question: can personal needs or desires outweigh the rights of others?

Value-Free Choices

The idea that life can be carried on without reference to value guidelines represents the most extreme example of efforts to escape authoritarian mandates. A curious claim, possibly traceable to sociologist-philosopher Max Weber,[5] is that education can be value-free and that one can be motivated to learn without concern for meaning or the nature of outcomes.

Values Clarification

An organized effort to restore reflective inquiry into value choices was the values clarification movement that gained support under the leadership of such educators as Louis E. Raths and Sidney Simon.[6] The strategy, which is process-oriented with little attention given to the content of moral values, calls for students to make choices that reflect their preferences for different types of alternatives. Peer approval, consideration of consequences of choices, and comparison with choices made by others are integral to the process. Proponents of this procedure argue that it provokes students to think about what they believe, prefer, or need. No claim is made that the approach helps to develop a desirable moral value structure; in fact, many of those who use this approach in schools argue that morality cannot be taught. Critics suggest that this process offers only superficial classroom exercises which may, in fact, add to the current value confusion (see Chapter 7).

Cognitive Moral Development

Kohlberg, an authority on moral psychology, is the originator of the cognitive moral development approach.[7] His research on the moral maturation of children and youth has been carried on at Harvard University over the past twenty years with a wide range of subjects. Out of these studies have come six defined stages of moral development that illustrate how people respond to moral mandates. Stage one, a primitive level, is one of obedience and punishment. In stage two, reciprocity, or cooperation through trade-offs with parents and teachers, is the predominant pattern. The good-boy/nice-girl, peer and parent approval, is the behavior pattern in stage three. Law and order, based on convictions of right and wrong, is the fourth stage; social contracts, the fifth; and the making of personal judgments about universal ethical principles is the sixth and highest stage of human responses. Research of this type is concerned mostly with theories about why people choose right over wrong. The focus is primarily on process, with little attention being given to the content of value decisions. Such knowledge, however, is most useful in helping teachers and parents to understand the level of maturity specific pupils have reached.

Human Needs Hierarchy

Another scientific approach to identifying value choices concerns the types and order of needs human beings confront. Maslow has been a pioneer in this effort.[8] He divides needs into lower-order and higher-order categories with values such as love, competence, and self-actualization accorded to the higher order while subsistence requirements, i. e., safety and security, are assigned to the lower-order type. Such rankings use the concept of needs as more or less interchangeable with that of value. The focus is on the necessary requirements for survival and maximum enjoyment of life.

Because human needs, the basic ones at least, tend to cross cultural boundary lines, this approach to valuing has positive implications for a cross-cultural morality perspective.

Value Analysis

The approach to valuing, called value analysis, [9] is a systematic process of rational inquiry into the values one considers desirable in relationship to those that others feel to be desirable. The aim is to provide a clear grasp of universally accepted values. After a logical analysis of human goals, each individual formulates his own value structure, the parts or premises of which are seen to be congruous with universal reality. Thus, the approach of value analysis makes the distillation of cross-cultural moral agreement its central objective. The purpose is to help individuals to achieve levels of reflection and commitment that cause actions to be based not on momentary feelings but, rather, on universal moral values.

Identifying Cross-cultural Values

Identified and discussed briefly below are examples of major categories that might together comprise one's value structure. These have been drawn from the research of Rokeach [10], Kohlberg [11], Maslow [12], Baier and Rescher [13], Raths [14], Simon [15], Dillman and Christenson, [16] as well as from the accumulated data collected by the Century III Foundation. [17] The terminology used to designate the cross-cultural value areas is that most typical of these studies. Attention is called to the fact that the majority of subjects studied were citizens of the United States, a nation where freedom, individual dignity, possession of property, and free enterprise are cherished values. Hence, assumptions drawn may have some degree of bias that such perspectives support. However the population studied was representative of various racial, ethnic, and religious groups. Given such limitations, these value perspectives are judged to have cross-cultural applications for the teaching of moral values that are basic to individual needs and social survival and that are relatively free from controversy.

Preservation and Fulfillment of Life

A universal need is to preserve and to fulfill human life, particularly if it is one's own. This has been found to be central in value structures accepted by individuals who have systematically analyzed their commitments. It requires the control of aggressive behavior, the assurance of health, self-acceptance, and intellectual, emotional, and physical development.

Sharing of Love

Without feelings of respect and affection among people—the sharing of love—human existence becomes meaningless in any culture. Thus, love prompts the provision of protection and nurture for the young, it provides security and feelings of self-worth, and contributes to mutual respect among people.

Need to Communicate

With group life comes the need to communicate. As information is exchanged, the necessity for accuracy and honesty becomes a moral mandate. For this reason, honesty is a cherished behavior in all groups that have formulated rules for moral behavior.

Satisfaction of Curiosity

Human beings have the rational mental capacities to explore cause and effect relationships. The will to discover meaning becomes an inescapable compulsion. As a result, the right to explore, to reason, to test assumptions, in short, to learn, ranks high as a category from which moral postulates are drawn.

Craving for Freedom

With enlightenment comes awareness of the precious nature of human freedom. The need and desire for self-actualization, to function as an independent person—to be free from coercive domination or persecution by others—is evidently a universal value.

Necessity for Accountability

Integrity, responsibility, dependability, justice—all are terms used to indicate the need in any social group for individuals to be accountable for their own actions.

The Use of Energy

The channeling of human energy toward a desired outcome is a valuing procedure which transcends culture. All activities and endeavors in which the human species is involved are in some way directed toward a specific outcome, and it is this procedure which determines respective morality systems. However, as Chapter 2 indicated, what is acceptable as an endeavor varies greatly from culture to culture—but the use of energy to generate the activity or event or idea is an inherent part of all cultures.

Concluding Statement

Every good teacher identifies appropriate objectives for instruction. Such goals are based on carefully chosen educational priorities. They are, it is hoped, in harmony with the total school/community value structure.   To assure such congruity, the logical first step for a teacher is the analysis of the values that predominate in the school and within the community it serves.   A common ground can usually be found by identifying those that have cross-cultural acceptance.   These, in turn, can form the basis for moral education.

The chart on the following page shows that it is desirable to have either a hierarchy of values, as Maslow suggested, or a system for analyzing values that allows for individual and pluralistic differences. With such approaches, the focus is upon *both* the process and the content, creating a more visible and natural cross-cultural impact and allowing for the creation of goals that serve individual and societal needs.

Figure 1
APPROACHES TO VALUING
Key Characteristics

APPROACH	RESULT OF THE APPROACH	REASON FOR THE APPROACH	FOCUS	CROSS-CULTURAL EMPHASIS	SOCIAL SURVIVAL USEFULNESS	SOME LEADING SPOKESMEN
Traditional Authoritarian	Reliance upon prescribed rules	Supreme Power or Wisdom	Content	None — High	High for sub-group	Religious leaders
Cultural Relativism	Reliance upon enforced laws	Cultural mores and laws	Content	None	High for sub-group	Rescher Baier
Situation Ethics	A flexible value system	Individual situations	Process	Some possible	Low	Fletcher
Value Free	Value confusion	None	None	None	None	Weber Marcuse
Values Clarification	Personal and peer preferences	Situational and personal desires	Process	Some possible	Low	Raths Simon
Cognitive Moral Development	Identifiable stages of moral development	Research evidence	Process	Some possible	Some to high—at stage 6	Kohlberg
Human Needs Hierarchy	Categories of preferred values	Physical and emotional needs	Process and content	High	High—defines goals	Rokeach Maslow
Value Analysis	A system to analyze value choices	Cross-cultural responses to value questions	Process and content	High	High—personal commitments	Century III Foundation

[1]Daniel Yankelovich, *The New Morality* (New York: McGraw-Hill Book Co., 1974), p. v.

[2]Kurt Baier and Nicholas Rescher, *Values and the Future* (New York: The Free Press, 1971), p. v.

[3]Jacques Monod, *Chance and Necessity* (New York: Alfred A. Knopf, 1971), p. 176.

[4]Joseph Fletcher, *Situation Ethics* (Philadelphia: Westminster Press), 1966.

[5]Max Weber, *Gesammelte Aufsatze zur Soziologie und Sozialpolitik* (Tubingen: J. C. B. Mohr, 1924), pp. 32, 40, 127, 148, 401, 470—71, 501, 577.
Note: In referring to Weber's views, Leo Strauss commented: "Weber contended that his notion of a "value-free" or ethically neutral social science is fully justified by what he regarded as the most fundamental of all oppositions, namely, the opposition of the Is and the Ought, or the opposition of reality and norm or value." Leo Strauss, "Natural Right and the Distinction Between Facts and Values," in *Philosophy of the Social Sciences,* ed. Maurice Natanson (New York: Random House, 1963), p. 424.

[6]See: Sidney B. Simon, et al., *Values Clarification* (New York: Hart Publishing Co., 1972), pp. 13—22.

[7]Lawrence Kolberg, "A Cognitive-Development Approach to Moral Edcuation " *The Humanist* (November-December, 1972): pp. 13—16.

[8]Frank Goble, *The Third Force* (Pasadena, Calif.: Thomas Jefferson Research Center, 1970), p. 36 and A. H. Maslow, ed. *New Knowledge in Human Values* (New York: Harper, 1959).

[9]Century III Foundation, *Discover a Common Sense Moral Standard Via Value Analysis* (Oak Brook, Ill.: The Foundation, 1976), pp. 1—24.

[10]Milton Rokeach, *The Nature of Human Values* (New York: The Free Press, 1973).

[11]Lawrence Kohlberg, "The Cognitive-Developmental Approach to Moral Education," *Phi Delta Kappan,* (June, 1975): 670—76.

[12]Abraham H. Maslow, *The Psychology of Science* (New York: Harper & Row, 1966).

[13]Baier and Rescher, *op. cit.*

[14]Louis E. Raths, et al., *Values and Teaching* (Columbus, Ohio: Charles E. Merrill Publishing Co., 1966).

[15]Sidney B. Simon, et al., *Values Clarification* (New York: Hart Publishing Co., 1972).

[16]Don A. Dillman and James A. Christenson, "Toward the Assessment of Public Values," *Psychological* Abstracts (The American Sociological Association, August 30, 1972), pp. 206—10.

[17]Century III Foundation, *op. cit.*, pp. 1—24.

4

Moral Education in the Schools

Robert Church

The development of mass schooling in the United States was predicated on the notion that schools could be effective agents for inculcating morality in youngsters. The widespread support for public schooling that emerged after 1830 grew out of the public's recognition that new ways of creating moral order had to be found that were applicable in an increasingly urbanized and ethnically and economically diverse society. By the middle of the nineteenth century, the public came to expect schools to train youth in ways that would assure such order and has been demanding ever since that public schools provide in one form or another "moral education" for their students. The spokespersons for the public schools have constantly reaffirmed the schools' commitment to, and effectiveness in, providing that "moral education." Without that commitment to moral education, there would have been little support for public education.

The schools' commitment to moral education has always, to a greater or lesser degree, conflicted with other expectations of schools shared by the public and by professional educators. The promises of democracy and equality and, especially the commitment to fostering religious, ethnic, and cultural pluralism that many groups have argued is implied in the Declaration of Independence and the Constitution, have made the provision of moral education a far more complex endeavor than the school leaders and their supporters originally suspected. Definitions of morality often lie at the very heart of what distinguishes ethnic, religious, and cultural groups from one another. Thus the public schools have had to seek ways of teaching morality without offending the values of minority groups. Most often, educators have tried to identify some kind of common morality, the tenets of which have been shared by all groups and peoples. This "common morality" has often seemed so amorphous and watered-down that it is not an adequate guide to correct behavior. The search for a common morality has also led schools to emphasize what might be called a negative morality: educators have apparently thought that a series of "do nots," a kind of Ten Commandments moral code devoid of references to how positively to live a moral life, is most palatable to most groups and appears most effective to the tax-payers who expect the schools to educate the young morally.

A second area of major conflict between moral education and the other purposes of the school has been that between the schools' commitment to affecting moral behavior and their dedication to improving intellectual skills. Through most of the period that we will be surveying, moral behavior was thought to spring more from the will, the heart, and the emotions than from reason or rationality. Educators have had much difficulty melding the intellectual functions of the schools with the schools' moral purposes. Few argued that the school should have only one purpose, but all were uncomfortable at the divergence between the schools' commitment to both intellectual development and moral inculcation. This discomfort was magnified by a tendency to consider intellectual training as a value-free, neutral endeavor to which most of the interest groups that make up America could not object. Moral education exhibited just the opposite qualities—its effectiveness depended on its being value-laden.

The historian finds a recurrent pattern in the institutionalization of moral education in the public schools of the United States: educators, pressured by the public to "teach" morality and pressured by law and conscience to respect pluralism, have worked to find a mode of moral education that takes on more and more of the qualities of value-free intellectual training. They have sought to sidestep the issue of which set of moral values should be taught by arguing that they are teaching morality when they teach children how to reason about morality. The appeal of teaching youngsters how to think rather than what to do has been nearly irresistible in the public schools because it promised to blend education's academic and moral purposes without offending cultural minorities. But that appeal has never been strong enough to overcome finally the belief that moral behavior results from will or emotion, rather than from reason. Few have been entirely convinced that the person who knows what is right will do what is right; that the child who is taught to think in order to discover the proper behavior will, upon discovering it, behave properly. The schools have been unable to resolve this dilemma.

This chapter will describe how educators sought to design an academic institution that could, in a pluralist society, offer effective moral education that would in fact affect behavior. Our focus will be on the century that began with the rise of the common school in the United States. A word about how "moral" and "moral education" are used in this chapter is in order. We will be using those terms as the historical actors used them. Readers should remember that only recently, if at all, have Americans felt able to segregate preparation for moral living into a portion of the developmental process and into a portion of the school day. Until recently, everything that a school did was supposed to contribute to the moral development of the child. (This is one reason why educators had so much trouble justifying intellectual training, for its relation to the moral development of children was not always readily apparent.) If anything that a school did, did not so contribute, the school should cease doing it. The public school existed to make better citizens "better," meaning "moral." Our definition of moral,

therefore, cannot be much more specific than what social and
educational leaders meant by "better"; when we refer to
moral education, we refer to the myriad ways that schools in
various periods have attempted to make youngsters into
"better" people.

Readers should also recognize the audacity of the public
schools' commitment to moral education, especially in the
nineteenth century. The schools accepted, indeed, sought,
responsibility for doing in a public, equitable way what had
for generations been done privately in family, church, and
local community. The schools assumed responsibility for
making political determinations as to what was to be considered "better"—the schools took up the task of finding a
common morality to fit a very diverse people. How inter-
esting, and, indeed, ironic, it is that in a nation founded on
the premise that the "people" are far better, more moral than
government, a nation founded in distrust of the inevitable
corruption of governmental power should, a mere half
century after its founding, allow governmental institutions
such as schools to take responsibility for defining and inculcating morality in the people. In agreeing to be agencies of
moral education, schools promised much; they have been
able to deliver little. The current resurgence of interest in
moral education cannot look to the past for guidance in
solving the problems of how effectively to teach morality
in public schools. But an understanding of past attempts at
"moral education" can familiarize people interested in this
area with the problems entailed in those attempts and perhaps introduce some healthy skepticism into the discussion
about whether moral education in a public institution is
either possible or desirable.

Moral Education and the Common Schools

The primary motivation for establishing comprehensive
systems of common schools dedicated to educating every
child in the United States at no direct charge to that child or

his family was the growing fear that urbanization, industrial-
ization, and immigration were creating moral disorder in
society. Raising children properly had always been a
problem, of course, but until the second quarter of the nineteenth century, most social leaders in the United States felt
that society could safely depend on family, church, and a
closely knit community to do so. Those who worried about
whether each new generation would mature into moral
adulthood took comfort from the expectation that most
children would pursue their parents' callings within their
parents' community. This set of social circumstances would
more than adequately discipline these new generations.
Children would remain at home or very close to home under
some form of parental discipline well into young adulthood,
and the church and the inquisitive community would be sure
to continue the discipline throughout that person's life. In
the small community, very little that an individual did
escaped the curious eyes of neighbors, the village elders, or
the local parson—none of whom hesitated for an instant to
correct an individual deviation. This form of social discipline
worked only imperfectly, even in colonial America, as there
was, for the time, an extraordinary amount of movement of
young people away from parental and community discipline.
Parental discipline worked most effectively when parents had
something—usually land or social position—to give to their
children. In a country with abundant land and opportunity,
children had little to gain by waiting for their parents to give
them what they could usually get for themselves with relatively little effort. This form of discipline was thought to
work tolerably well, however, until the second quarter of the
nineteenth century.

With the opening of the trans-Appalachian west after the
War of 1812 and the creation of efficient commercial canal
and railway links among the regions of the country, the character of the United States began to change. These social
changes destroyed the confidence that men's natural pen-
chant for evil or immorality would be automatically held in

check by family, church, and community. First of all, people, and especially young people, moved around more, away from parents and from the communities in which they were raised, and thus away from traditional disciplinary systems. Large numbers migrated to cities—in 1800, only about 6 percent of Americans lived in cities over 2,500 people; in 1830 the figure had risen to less than 9 percent, but in 1860 almost one in every five Americans lived in an urban place. In 1976, when most Americans live in metropolitan areas, these figures appear quite small, but we should recognize that to the Americans of the time, urbanization was proceeding at a fabulous rate. Cities deeply frightened Americans. As early as 1809, Governor DeWitt Clinton of New York described the evils of urban life in New York City and its pernicious effect on young people. "Great cities are at all times the nurseries and hotbeds of crime," Clinton wrote. "Bad men from all quarters repair to them, in order to obtain the benefit of concealment, and to enjoy in a superior degree the advantages of rapine and fraud. And the dreadful examples of vice, which are presented to youth, and the alluring forms in which it is arrayed, connected with a spirit of extravagance and luxury, the never-failing attendant of great wealth and extensive business, cannot fail of augmenting the mass of moral depravity."[1] Urbal living threatened the established forms of social discipline: cities were vast impersonal places where people neither knew nor cared for each other as they had in the smaller villages of colonial America. Urban dwellers acquired an unprecedented and frightening privacy that undermined the traditional means of social discipline. A person could live in an urban tenement or boarding house without even knowing his neighbors or being known by them. Without such knowledge, there could be no effective interpersonal supervision.

Territorial expansion and improved transporation and technology encouraged rapid growth of American manufacturing—initially in cotton and iron and then in scores of other fields. An ever-increasing working class of factory operatives was needed to serve this industrial growth. Social leaders perceived these operatives as quite different from the largely agricultural Americans of an earlier generation. They threatened moral order because they owned no property and thus had no "stake" in society, and because their tedious, long-houred indoor factory labor was likely to degrade them physically, psychologically, and morally. They were thought to lack initiative, self-control, and responsibility. Because they were likely to bequeath these traits to their children, they presented a perpetual threat to social order.

During the middle of the nineteenth century, immigration intensified significantly, particularly from Ireland and southern Germany—areas of Europe that had previously contributed few immigrants. Unlike earlier generations of immigrants, these aliens did not blend inconspicuously into the native American population. They were largely Catholic in an almost totally Protestant country; the Germans spoke a strange language (and many considered the English that the Irish spoke rather strange too). Native Americans thought them to be more financially and morally impoverished than they recalled earlier immigrants having been. The threat that these strangers presented to social stability was heightened by the fact that they tended to congregate in cities and to work in factories.

These circumstances made it impossible to trust any longer the traditional means of enforcing social discipline and insuring the proper moral instruction of the young. The story of the common schools' establishment as an alternative means of instilling moral discipline has been adequately recounted many times and need not be repeated here. Just as society was establishing public police forces and asylums as governmental agencies to maintain order among adults, it developed a system of universal schooling to serve as a form of preventative police to insure moral order among prospective adults. Horace Mann, a leader of the common school movement, argued that mass schooling, properly implemented, would make "nine-tenths of the crimes in the penal

code . . . obsolete; [abridge] the long catalogue of human
ills . . .; men would walk more safely by day; every pillow
would be more inviolable by night; property, life, and character held by a stronger tenure; all rational hopes respecting
the future brightened."[2]

This was a tall order for the schools to fulfill, but they set
about doing so with immense self-confidence. How did they
propose to effect such startling moral improvments among
their charges? One prime way was by preparing them to read
moral books. The theory that children should be taught to
read so that they can learn how to live morally, and thus
maintain social order, had a long history. From the beginnings of colonial society, leaders insisted that children learn
to read in order to be able to understand the rules and regulations contained in the Bible. The famous Massachusetts
law of 1647 rationalized compulsory schooling by identifying as "one chief object of that old deluder, Satan," the
attempt "to keep men from the knowledge of the Scrip-
tures."[3]   Literacy promoted morality; illiteracy, evil. But
colonial educational laws were honored more in the breach
than in the observance; most colonial children learned to read
at home, if at all.

In the revolutionary era, the justification for a literate
populace changed from a religious to a political orientation.
Thomas Jefferson stated, "If a nation expects to be ignorant
and free, in a state of civilization, it expects what never was
and never will be."[4]   Democracy could not work without
literate people capable of reading about and understanding
public issues. Only a literate public could resist the blandish-
ments of demagogues, considered to be the greatest threat to
democracy because of their ability to persuade people on
emotional rather than on rational grounds.   Despite the
often-stated need for literacy in a democracy during the early
decades of the republic, most political information available
to the mass of people was transmitted orally.

The relation between reading and the moral order
changed once more by 1830, largely because traditional
forms of social control and the direct contact between

leaders and those being led began to disintegrate. In a hetero-geneous, complex society, ways of communicating moral strictures had to be found that were more efficient than the older, word-of-mouth means. As social distance between classes increased after 1830, power and influence became more centralized. Family, church, and community could no longer be trusted effectively to inculcate moral behavior orally. Consequently, social leaders increasingly depended on the printed word to influence the moral behavior of the lower social classes and of groups distant from centers of in-fluence. There had to be a guarantee that the intended recip-ients of those messages were capable of receiving them. They had to be taught to read. Reading was far more crucial to social health than it had been before. This time action had to match the rhetorical commitment to literacy. Reading, therefore, went hand-in-hand with the mission of the com-mon schools—common because they were supposed to pro-vide the same education for all children, because they taught the common branches of the curriculum, and because they transmitted a common morality. People felt that common-ality or consistency was better achieved through a written moral code than through an oral one, and that for children, teaching a moral curriculum with more up-to-date and expli-cit illustrations than those contained in the Bible would be effective.

In response to these needs, the common schools built their moral curriculum around readers such as those pub-lished by William Holmes McGuffey. McGuffey's readers, first published in the 1830s and used in virtually every school in the United States between the 1840s and the end of the century, were compendia of stories, Biblical passages, and poetry selected for style, information, range of authors, and interest, and designed "to exert a decided and health-ful moral influence."[5] McGuffey and his publishers con-sistently chose stories explicitly suffused with Victorian sentimentality and mid-nineteenth century "materialistic morality" in which those who chose to do the right thing always received some sort of material reward—money or a job— while those who chose incorrectly were explicitly punished—often quite severely. His books transmitted an authoritative moral code.

Henry Steele Commager has suggested that widespread use of those readers laid a groundwork of common allusion and reference among nineteenth-century Americans.[6] I would suggest that their wide use also made them an effective channel through which to transmit and maintain a common set of moral values and definitions. Such a common moral code based on the written word had decided advantages in a complex society experiencing tremendous social and geographic mobility. Parental moral strictures carried less weight as one moved away from the range of their voices; the pressures exerted by the local community could not influence those who had moved elsewhere. Although the basic moral beliefs from family to family or from community to community were similar—moving to new surroundings did not throw one into a different moral environment—the common basic morality was expressed in a variety of ways. McGuffey identified and standardized this basic morality. His readers were, in a sense, a mass-produced moral code, and like so much else that is mass-produced, they suppressed different local flavors in favor of an unvarying, homogenous morality equally applicable in Burlington, Vermont, and Burlington, Iowa. McGuffey gave the country a single language with which to discuss morality; moral strictures heard in one's native community were reinforced in other communities with the same examples and words. McGuffey depersonalized and standardized the moral code; such universalization was thought quite important in a society undergoing such movement, fragmentation, and recoalescence. Because public school supporters perceived that the possibility existed for using the written word to control the moral behavior of those leaving the orbit of the traditional controls of the stable community, they demanded that schools teach children to read the right things. Correct reading habits would insure proper moral behavior, they thought.

One should note carefully the demand that students be taught to read the right things, for mass literacy is a two-edged sword from the moral leader's viewpoint. The leader gains some control because he has additional media with which to influence behavior, but he also loses considerable influence because literate people can use their ability to read anything they choose. Therefore, one not only had to teach people how to read but also to teach them to read the right things. Nothing was gained if those taught to read in fact read material that urged them to contradict desirable moral behavior. Therefore, it was crucial to develop reading taste as well as reading skills. McGuffey achieved considerable success in defining what was generally accepted as proper literature through his published selections. Moreover, he and the schoolmen hoped that children trained to read such carefully selected reading material would continue to seek that kind of reading as adults.

The advocates of using reading to affect moral behavior in that day never clearly described the relation between reading and subsequent moral action, but they were convinced that reading moral lessons would influence behavior. McGuffey and his imitators obviously believed and expected their work to affect behavior by appealing to sentiments of fear and greed. They appear to have attributed far more power to the written word than we would today; they even seem to have considered it more powerful than the spoken word. Their views might best be understood as a parallel to current views of how much more powerful new media such as television and other audio-visual tools are than the print medium. In 1830, of course, books were not new, but their wide and cheap circulation was.

By the second third of the nineteenth century, the written word was the modern, efficient way to affect behavior. People then were as willing to believe in the new medium's power over emotions without ever receiving a very clear explanation of how it worked as today we agree that television is influential, although its influence has not yet been completely clarified. In any case, it is clear that school leaders did not expect readers to interpose any substantial intellectual or rational activity between reading a moral message and carrying out a moral action.

McGuffey's series and the other readers contained rules and directives to be translated directly into action. No reasoning upon those rules was necessary because reading was supposed to influence the emotions and the will. Perhaps, that was why so much of the code was packaged as fiction during this period. Mass schooling was also expected to influence moral behavior by developing mental discipline in young people. The doctrine of mental discipline postulated that students should be forced to study difficult subjects at length because the skills they then acquired would easily transfer to other, less rigorous subjects. We are concerned here not with the "transfer of training" aspect of mental discipline, but rather with the significant moral implications inherent in it. Advocates believed that the skills, such as perseverance, developed by rigorous academic training would directly transfer to the development of correct moral behavior. Children who were forced to assume responsibility, to accept arduous tasks, and to resist the temptation to engage in pleasurable activities that interfered with other obligations, would mature morally and behave properly as adults. Mental discipline would develop self-control, a vital component of the moral code of the mid-nineteenth century, which emphasized social and moral order. In the case of mental discipline, as of reading, there was little connection made between the intellectual content of pedagogy and the desired moral outcomes. To promoters of mental discipline, it made no difference what subject was studied, as long as it was difficult. A subject was considered difficult because it was complex and hard to memorize, not because it required significant intellectual endeavor. Mental discipline was valuable to moral education since it trained the will, not the intellect.

Educators also agreed that schools could influence students' moral behavior in areas that were not academic. While agreeing that schools should play a parental role in the moral training of children, educators disagreed on the exact character of that role: those who identified moral training with the image of the stern father (an angry and unknowable God) believed that the schools should suppress incorrect behavior, while those who identified moral training with the softer, gentler, loving mother image (an approachable, loveable Christ-figure) insisted that teachers assume a maternal posture toward their students, a position that contributed to the feminization of the teaching force in the mid-nineteenth century. Most schoolmen in the first half of the nineteenth century probably believed in the inherent "evil" of young children and in the necessity of using the fear of punishment to train them to resist their inclination to be mischievous. A group of Boston schoolmasters, critical of Horace Mann's flexible and gentle approach to discipline and authority in the classroom, endorsed these views of their disciplinary role:

> The first step which a teacher must take, I do not mean *in* his course of moral education, but before he is prepared to enter that course, is to obtain the entire, unqualified submission of his school to his *authority*. We often err when designing to exert a moral influence, by substituting throughout our whole system persuasion for power; but we soon find that the gentle winning influence of moral suasion, however beautiful in theory, will often fall powerless upon the heart, and we then must have authority, to fall back upon, or all is lost. . . . However men may differ in their theories of human nature, it is pretty generally agreed by those who have tried the experiment, that neither school nor family can be preserved . . . by eloquence and argument alone. There must be authority. The pupils may not often feel it. But they *must know that it is always at hand*, and the pupils must be taught to submit to it as simple *authority*. The subjection of the governed to the will of one man, in such a way as the expression of his will must be the final decision of every question, is the only government that will answer in school or in family. A government not of persuasion, not of reasons assigned, not of the will of the majority, but of the will of the one who presides.[7]

Consequently, children were often disciplined physically. Schoolmen simply imported a method of discipline and punishment commonly used in the home and usually unrelated to intellectual development. Concurrently, a few theorists in the fields of human development and education argued that children were born with strong tendencies toward "good" behavior. They disagreed with those who insisted that schools should affect moral behavior by physically suppressing "evil" tendencies in children, and instead agreed that schools should cultivate and nurture the potentially positive traits. Toward these goals, they supported a gentler and more subtle form of discipline, but one that was no less manipulative. Believing that children acted correctly to earn the love of their parents or teachers, they rewarded good behavior by giving love and punished incorrect behavior by withdrawing it. Whether particular educators agreed about the exact nature of discipline and reward in the schools is less significant than that both groups sought to influence the moral behavior of children through appealing directly to the emotions of love and fear. Neither group, however, related their efforts directly to the curricula of the schools.

With only minor changes applicable to varied local conditions, these approaches to moral education that appeared soon after the establishment of the common school system endured through the rest of the century. It appears that the motherly approach gradually gained more adherents, but certainly was far from dominant by 1900. Between 1850 and 1885, the tenets that had justified the moral educational value of mental discipline were also used to justify the moral value of industrial training—especially in reform schools and among freedmen after the Civil War. Neither plaiting straw hats nor cutting nails ten to twelve hours a day taught delinquents a productive, marketable skill, reform school operators admitted, but it did teach them to work hard and conscientiously which was the essence of moral action, particularly for children who had behavior problems.[8]

Surprisingly little controversy surrounded the concept of moral education in the nineteenth century, and nearly all that surfaced publicly was initiated by groups who felt that moral education in the schools, in striving for universality, had become too soft and amorphous. Catholics formed the most vocal opposition. They objected to the absence of commentary and annotation in the King James Version of the Bible, which was the only version acceptable to the boards of education that sought both to stimulate Catholic attendance in the public schools and to improve their morality. Refused the opportunity to use their own version of the Bible, Catholics established their own parochial school systems that were more directive in their moral teaching than were the public schools. Although less vociferous and demanding, other religious groups also objected to the common schools' lack of directiveness. They argued that moral education could be effective only if it were tied directly to the moral code of a particular faith or sect.[9]

Moral education, therefore, was very much a part of the purpose of the nineteenth century schools, as they replaced the family, church, and community as the prime agency to insure that children were raised properly. In large part, the schools relied upon the traditional means of family discipline—manipulation of fear and love, for example—in influencing the young. Educators almost always stressed their opportunities to influence moral behavior by directly affecting the individual's emotions and will rather than reasoning faculties.[10]

Moral Training in the Progressive Era

Led by John Dewey, educators at the beginning of the twentieth century made a concerted attempt to link moral education with the intellectual or academic purposes of the schools. They argued that a close tie between rational capabilities and moral behavior existed and that the school could, therefore, influence the second by improving the first. This argument drew upon a definition of morality that differed significantly from that which dominated educational theory during the era of the common school movement. To Dewey and his colleagues, morality was relativistic in assuming that no single, identifiable, predetermined moral code was adequate to guide behavior in the modern world. They agreed that the definition of moral behavior depended more upon the circumstances in which the individual existed than upon a code of a priori rules. Correct moral behavior therefore required the individual to think rationally about his situation and then to act accordingly. Dewey and his supporters consequently called upon the schools both to teach a mode of reasoning about making correct moral decisions and to provide students with sufficient information about society to guide their thinking.

The extent of Dewey's influence on the schools is quite problematic in this area, as in others. Our discussion, therefore, must center on his ideas rather than on their implementation by classroom teachers simply because we do not know to what extent or in what fashion they were carried out. Dewey believed that thinking and action were systems of problem solving: when individuals were confronted with new situations or choices where previous rules did not apply, they first thought and then acted. Immensely affected by what he perceived as continual change in the modern world, Dewey believed that individuals would be constantly confronted with new situations that then would require innovative thought and action. Everyone had to be expected to develop his own rules in modern society.

Like most moralists who are eager to see each person develop an entirely separate moral code, Dewey believed that a mechanism for checking the moral validity of certain actions and of reaching some sort of agreement to what was proper behavior had to be developed. The first step toward this goal was to develop a consensus among individuals about the process of determining the relative value of moral decisions. The consensus that Dewey believed would allow individuals with differing opinions ultimately to reach agreement was to be based upon scientific rationality. As did many social philosophers during the Progressive era, Dewey believed that science and the scientific method would solve all human problems. Disagreement and conflict, he thought, evolved from misunderstanding of the situation under consideration and therefore did not result from basic emotional or political differences among individuals or groups. Conflict could always be resolved, consequently, if the adversaries agreed to submit their differences to scientific scrutiny. Schools had to train children to employ the scientific method of resolving disputes, for that method could develop unity and moral consensus. Although individuals made their own moral decisions, agreement and commonality emerged from consistent and unanimous reliance upon the scientific method. Without too much oversimplification, this argument also can be related to Dewey's pragmatism: the truth of a conclusion or the morality of an action is determined primarily by how well the conclusion explains actual events or how successful the action is in the real world. Intellectual training, in this case, in the skills necessary to assess the effects of an action, was thus a necessary aspect of moral education.

Morality for Dewey was a social decision: intelligent moral action could not occur without individuals' possessing what Dewey called "social intellegence—the power of observing and comprehending social situations—and social power—trained capacities of control—at work in the service of social interest and aims."[11] Social intelligence could be taught as part of the school's regular academic curriculum, for in the concept of social intelligence, knowledge and morality went hand in hand. Indeed, Dewey claimed that all subjects should be taught in a fashion that would bring "the child to realize the social scene of actions." If subjects were not taught in this way, they did not belong in the school because they encouraged—at least implicity—self-absorption,

exclusiveness, and competition. [12] Dewey continually argued
that the nineteenth-century school taught anti-social selfish-
ness by recalling the rooms full of children studying silently
and alone at their desks, and emphasized that those schools
treated morality as an identifiable code of rules and duties—
phrased as negative "thou shalt nots"—that applied only to
certain aspects of the child's life. Dewey argued instead that
(1) all thinking is done in the service of action—that it is
functional, (2) that all action occurs in a social setting, and
(3) that moral and ethical relations are crucial to any social
setting. Therefore, educators "must take the child as a
member of society in the broadest sense, and demand for and
from the schools whatever is necessary to enable the child
intelligently to recognize all his social relations and take his
part in sustaining them."[13] Proper social behavior and sustaining social relations were the essence of morality. Therefore, Dewey concluded, "there is no fact which throws light
upon the constitution of society, there is no power whose
training adds to social resourcefulness ... that is not
moral."[14] Moral education could be furthered then by or-
ganizing a curriculum so that each of its aspects contributed
to "the formation of habits of social imagination and conception." [15]

One accomplished this goal in a number of ways. History
and geography were to be taught in such a way as to illu-
minate the child's present and local social situations rather
than as a compendia of facts about distant lands and times.
English was to be taught primarily as a means of increasing
communication, and thus social intercourse, among people.
Mathematics and home economics were to be taught in ways
that would demonstrate to children that the skills they acquired were applicable to their immediate social situation.
To encourage this, the classroom and the school were con-
verted as far as possible into actual communities. Students
studying arithmetic, for example, could then apply their skills
immediately in the school store; in the Gary, Indiana, school
system, which Dewey admired, students studied home eco-

nomics to prepare lunches for their classmates. Teachers in Gary managed the classrooms so that students spent more time working with each other in cooperative social endeavors than they did sitting at their desks working selfishly on their own work. Dewey thus defined moral education as any way of increasing the child's understanding of how a complex industrial society worked, of the importance of cooperation, and of the extent of social interdependence.

For the first time in the history of mass schooling in the United States, an educator had combined the requirements for transmitting knowledge and for developing moral education into a single process. Dewey was able to do so largely because he, and middle-class American society between 1890 and 1920, strongly believed in the power of rationality to guide behavior. Although he appears to have recognized the gap between knowing what is right and actually doing it, Dewey, and his colleagues, did not consider it a very important problem before 1920. He accepted the notion that children had a natural instinct to work cooperatively and to sustain social relations. If the schools rewarded this behavior, it would continue into adulthood. In general, social philosophers during the Progressive era had a great deal of faith that simple recognition of a problem and agreement about its proper solution would lead to its elimination. Once it was identified, the right solution would be implemented. Educators therefore were convinced that correct moral behavior, in terms of emotions and the will, was natural and presented no serious problem; teachers needed only to improve their students' social understanding to insure that everyone would act properly.

While Dewey's position on moral education could be interpreted as flexible and non-authoritarian, it appears that he and his colleagues had definite ideas about proper moral behavior. Knowledge about social interdependence does not necessarily result in specific conclusions about what is proper behavior in social situations. Today we accept that people with equal objective knowledge about a social situation will conclude that quite different responses are morally appropriate. Dewey's position can be interpreted in this way, and has been, particularly by teachers who, when criticized that they neglected moral instruction, claimed that they supplied information or knowledge with which individuals could make their own moral decisions rather than simple rules for correct behavior.

I doubt, however, that Dewey and his colleagues really felt that they were offering a flexible, individualistic alternative to codified morality. In the context of the confidence Americans during the Progressive era had in science and rationality as a source of certainty, another interpretation is more probable. What was discovered scientifically or rationally was "correct." Science was a way of settling disputes, resolving conflicts, and discovering certain truths. Providing knowledge and developing analytical skills in school was not done with the anticipation that individuals would make different moral decisions in social situations, but simply to let them make their own decisions with every confidence that with the proper information before them, everyone would make identical, correct decisions.

Surely Dewey's position was more liberal and open to a changing moral environment than were those of educators in the nineteenth century. Dewey was able to be liberal and still receive a wide hearing because the public generally had faith in rationality as a source of unity and commonality and because the Progressive era was a unique period in American history. Then, Americans were optimistic about the political and social future of their nation, and the conflicts that are so often exacerbated by hard times were relatively suppressed. It was widely agreed that social conditions could and should be improved and the remedies were sufficiently vague to attract support from many varied groups. During the era of the common school movement, there had been optimism, but it was coupled with an overriding fear among the social leaders about the deterioration of values and morality. Consequently, they imposed an inflexible, tight, directive, authoritarian moral code on people in order to reestablish America's moral foundation. During the optimistic, bouyant, Progressive era, social leaders agreed that indeed there were problems but recognized that Americans were intelligent enough to solve them. A seemingly more open system of moral education was therefore acceptable, particularly because Americans were confident that such moral instruction would lead to common moral behavior.[16]

Trends in Moral Education Since World War I

The conditions that made possible Dewey's melding of the intellectual and moral aspects of public schooling did not survive World War I. Propaganda's successful appeal to the emotions and the popularization of Freud's theses about the controlling nature of the unconscious made the pre-war years' faith in the power of reason seem unjustified. Furthermore, the results of the war and the Progressive generation's failure to reform American society severely undermined the optimism that had characterized pre-war social philosophy. A visible increase in conflict among cultural and religious groups in the United States over the difinition of proper moral conduct also contributed to the deterioration of the confidence and optimism Americans had in their ability to eliminate serious disagreement. Schools were inevitably dragged into these conflicts, and a form of moral education, which emphasized the value of knowledge and the development of rational decision-making skills, became increasingly unpopular in a nation confronted by the vast and basic cultural and moral conflicts symbolized by the resurgence of the Ku Klux Klan, the Scopes Trial, and the Prohibition movement. Various groups and cultural organization wanted their specific and rigid codes taught in the schools. Once again, many identified morality with the emotions rather than with reason and once again expected schools to reach those emotions directly.

Educators were no clearer after 1920 about how to reach those emotions than they had been in the nineteenth century, but they did vigorously sift through a number of alternative approaches to influence their students' emotions. The various approaches ranged from the direct character training and life adjustment movements to dress and honor codes, chaperoned dances, and other formal extracurricular activities. Educators attempted explicity to harness peer pressure to control student behavior. School personnel usually retained Dewey's emphasis on the social context of morality but often engaged in a decidedly more heavy-handed socialization process than Dewey would have accepted. Educators attempted to teach children to fit in, to be liked, to adjust to social reality, to be content with what they had. With the promotion and expansion of these activities, the gap between developing the intellect and providing knowledge on the one hand and affecting moral behavior on the other increased greatly. Schools adapted many nineteenth-century methods —carefully selecting reading material to influence moral behavior most efficiently, and simulating the adult reward and punishment structure in the schools, for example. Perhaps the most orginal addition to the schools' repertoire was their skill in successfully manipulating their students' peer culture in order to control student behavior.

This subject deserves much attention and requires a significant amount of research, but there is sufficient evidence to support the hypothesis that the curricular and extracurricular projects that emphasized group cooperation implemented between the world wars increased the dependence of young people on the judgment and opinion of their peers as the most accurate measure of their social adjustment and success and thus made peer pressure the most important determinant of moral behavior in a child's life. Social commentators in the 1950s such as David Riesman and William H. Whyte confirmed the immense influence that peer pressure, supported and guided by the public schools, had on the behavior of the young. Neither peer pressure nor any of the other tools of an oral education used by the schools after 1920 were allied with the intellectual training carried out in the schools. Dewey's fragile marriage between moral and intellectual training had dissolved. Moral education or character training, remained the primary function of schooling and once again it was sharply differentiated from the schools' responsibility to develop intellectual skills.[17]

Since the 1950s, proponents of moral education have sought once again to couple the intellectual and moral training functions of the school. Their goal has been to develop a single unified purpose that will not offend religious and cultural groups. Current interest in and proposals for moral education that attempt to combine rigorous intellectual training with effective moral development must address the following questions: Do the proposed forms of moral education teach about morality or do they influence moral behavior? Can educators develop moral education that is vital and yet that is neither offensive to specific groups nor authoritarian in its implementation? These are the questions that have confronted educators for nearly a century and a half and have remained both unclarified and unsolved.

[1]Rena Vassar, ed., *Social History of American Education* (Chicago: Rand McNally, 1965), 1: p. 199.

[2]Mary T. P. Mann, *The Life and Works of Horace Mann* (Boston: 1891), 1: p. 142.

[3]The 1647 Massachusetts Bay education act is discussed in Lawrence A. Cremin, *American Education: The Colonial Experience, 1607–1783* (New York: Harper and Row, 1970), pp. 124–25.

[4]Thomas Jefferson to Col. Charles Yancey (6 Jan. 1816), quoted in Gordon C. Lee, ed., *Thomas Jefferson on Education* (New York:

Teachers College Press, 1961), p. 19; and Frederick Rudolph, ed., *Essays on Education in the Early Republic*, (Cambridge, Mass.: Harvard University Press, 1965).

[5]Henry Steele Commager, ed., *McGuffey's Fifth Eclectic Reader* (1879; New York: The New American Library, 1962), p. xv.

[6]Ibid., pp. x—xiv.

[7]Boston Schoolmasters, *Remarks on the Seventh Annual Report of the Honorable Horace Mann, Secretary of the Massachusetts Board of Education* (Boston, 1844), pp. 128—131.

[8]Robert L. Church and Michael W. Sedlak, *Education in the United States: An Interpretive History* (New York: The Free Press, 1976), Chapters 5—7.

[9]The Catholic school controversy and its relationship to nineteenth-century moral education is examined in Vincent P. Lannie, *Public Money and Parochial Education* (Cleveland: Case Western Reserve University Press, 1968); Carl F. Kaestle, *The Evolution of an Urban School System: New York City, 1750—1850* (Cambridge, Mass.: Harvard University Press, 1973); Diane Ravitch, *The Great School Wars: New York City, 1805—1973* (New York: Basic Books, 1974); and Church and Sedlak, *Education in the United States*, Chapter 6.

[10]This section on antebellum cultural conflict and moral education in the public schools has drawn extensively on Michael B. Katz, *The Irony of Early School Reform: Educational Innovation in Mid-Nineteenth Century Massachusetts* (Cambridge, Mass.: Harvard University Press, 1968), which includes an excellent introduction to the controversy over discipline and authority; Kaestle, *The Evolution of an Urban School System;* Stanley K. Schultz, *The Culture Factory: Boston Public Schools, 1789—1860* (New York: Oxford University Press, 1973); Church and Sedlak, *Education in the United States*, Chapters 3 and 4; and Bernard Wishy, *The Child and the Republic: The Dawn of Modern American Child Nurture* (Philadelphia: University of Pennsylvania Press, 1968), and Barbara Finkelstein, "Pedagogy as Intrusion: Teaching Values in Popular Primary Schools in the Nineteenth Century," *History of Childhood Quarterly*, XI (Winter, 1975), pp. 349-78, which examine child-raising practices during this period.

[11]John Dewey, *Moral Principles in Education* (Boston: Houghton Mifflin Co., 1909), p. 43.

[12]Ibid., p. 31.

[13]Ibid., pp. 8—9.

[14]Ibid., p. 43.

[15]Ibid., p. 41.

[16]This examination of moral training and educational progressivism is based on Lawrence Cremin, *The Transformation of the Schools: Progressivism in American Education, 1876—1957* (New York: Alfred A. Knopf, 1961); Edward Krug, *The Shaping of the American High School, 1880—1920* (Madison: University of Wisconsin Press, 1964); Joel Spring, *Education and the Rise of the Corporate State* (Boston: Beacon Press, 1972); Marvin Lazerson, *Origins of the Urban School: Public Education in Massachusetts, 1870—1915* (Cambridge, Mass.: Harvard University Press, 1971); Church and Sedlak, *Education in the United States*, Chapters 8—10; Clarence Karier, "Liberal Ideology and the Quest for Orderly Change," in Karier, et al., eds., *Roots of Crisis* (Chicago: Rand McNally, 1973), pp. 84—107; and the literature spawned by the current reinterpretation of John Dewey, which may be sampled in various issues of the *History of Education Quarterly* for 1975 and 1976.

[17]See, for example, David Riesman, *The Lonely Crowd* (New Haven, Conn.: Yale University Press, 1950); William H. Whyte, *The Organization Man* (New York: Simon and Schuster, 1956); C. Wright Mills, *White Collar: The American Middle Classes* (New York: Oxford University Press, 1951); Herbert J. Gans, *The Levittowners* (New York: Pantheon Books, 1967); Spring, *Education and the Rise of the Corporate State*; Edward Krug, *The Shaping of the American High School: Volume II, 1920—1941* (Madison: University of Wisconsin Press, 1972); and Church and Sedlak, *Education in the United States*, Chapter 12.

5

How Moral Values are Learned

John Lee
Susan Dye Lee

In some ways, writing about moral values would be well left to theologians or philosophers. The rest of us could stay with safer questions about teaching history or social studies, phonics or linguistics, sets or multiplication tables. Or we could be truly safe with penmanship, woodworking, and driver education.

The difficulty in writing about moral values is the back-of-the-mind feeling that one is expected to say which values should be taught and to provide a set of lesson plans for teaching them. If that is what you expect, then you should stop reading here. You won't find either in this chapter.

What will you find? First, there is a brief synopsis of what Freud had to say about the development of the super-ego or conscience. There is nothing you can do to influence most of what Freud says, but it should help you understand what has happened before the child got to your class. The second section is on Piaget's developmental psychology, with emphasis on what is called affective development. The usual report on Piaget deals with motor skills and intelligence; there is little of that here, but we have tried to pull together what he has said about morality. In the third section is a consideration of how values change—or, more often do not change—as a result of teacher behavior or of schooling. Most of this section is drawn from the work of social psychologists, and it provides several cues about how to teach in a manner calculated to influence moral learning.

These sections do not tell you how to teach morality, but they should cause you to ask yourself if you are taking advantage of some circumstances and approaches that might affect what students learn about moral knowledge, moral values, and moral conduct.

In a psychological sense, morality is a set of internalized standards or criteria for discriminating good behavior from bad. The acquisition of morality involves knowing, feeling, and acting—and then thinking about consequences. Moral knowledge provides the standards for judging conduct. Moral feelings decrease or enhance a sense of self-worth or self-esteem. Moral actions indicate the extent of agreement between moral knowledge and moral feelings.

Psychoanalytic Theory Of Moral Development

Sigmund Freud formulated a body of hypotheses that attempt to explain the origin, development, and function of an individual's mental life. These hypotheses, referred to as a psychoanalytic theory, are widely known and widely misunderstood. It is important, though, to understand the terminology of the hypotheses in order to comprehend the application of the theory on an individual's moral development.

In a broad sense, psychoanalytic theory attempts to explain how cultural heritage is acquired and internalized by each generation. In Freud's view, civilization is a special process mankind undergoes, a conflict in which demands of the individual for unlimited freedom are modified by the claims of society. The struggle between these two forces takes place within the unconscious, pitting instinct against a cultural heritage. This battle between nature and culture inheres in the very fact of culture, and is irreconcilable.

The Id, the Ego, and the Superego

Freud identifies three provinces in the psychical apparatus of a human being. The id, present at birth and throughout life, contains everything an individual inherits—above all, needs and instincts. The ego, which begins development at about six months, mediates between the id and the external world, it seeks pleasure and avoids pain. The superego begins development at about three years of age, and is the source of moral imperatives; it rewards and punishes when these imperatives are followed or disobeyed.

In the individual, as in civilization, the instincts of sexuality and aggression exist simultaneously. These instincts, according to Freud, are in an individual's id. The id might be characterized as being primitive, selfish, shameless, and unconscious. Also, love and death instincts exist simultaneously in the id, thereby exhibiting irrationality as one of its principle attributes.

Under the influence of the external world, a portion of the id develops into the ego, which becomes that part of the mental life whose responsibility is self-preservation. In relation to the id, the ego attempts to gain control over instinctual demands, deciding whether they will receive satisfaction, postponing satisfaction until time and circumstance are favorable, or suppressing some urges entirely. By mediating between the demands of the id and the realities of the enviroment, the ego functions to gain motor control for the infant, to use the senses to understand the environment, and to store memories of gratification and their means of achievement.

The third province of mankind's psychical apparatus, the superego, accounts for the way in which a sense of morality is internalized. To understand the manner in which this is carried out according to Freud's theory, one must understand the Oedipus complex. This refers to the conflict a child experiences as a result of ambivalent love/death wishes he feels towards his parents. During the Oedipal stage, at approximately thirty to thirty-six months of age, the child wishes to establish an exclusive love relationship with the opposite-sex parent. Simultaneously, the child envies the same-sex parent and wishes to eliminate that parent from the triangle.

Strong feelings surround the child's desires. They are as intense as any the individual will ever have and they manifest themselves in different ways, according to sex. Prior to the initiation of the Oedipal phase, girls and boys develop along similar lines. Both sexes have their strongest object relationships with the mother. With the appearance of genital desires, however, the essentially bisexual nature of children must come to grips with anatomical reality, and the psychic development of boys and girls ceases its parallel course. Each sex, therefore, experiences the Oedipal complex in a fundamentally different way.

As the Oedipus complex is resolved, the formation of the superego occurs. Previous to this phase, the child has no natural capacity to distinguish good from bad. Instead, the process of learning to deal with instinctual frustration produces in him a kind of proto-conscience. When insatiable infant demands are not wholly satisfied, the child not only experiences aggressive impulses, but also a sense of anxiety. He is helpless and is dependent on others for the gratification of his needs. If he loses the love of persons on whom he depends, he also loses their protection. According to Freud, "At the beginning, therefore, what is bad is whatever causes one to be threatened with loss of love."[1] Anxiety over the possible loss of love objects becomes the motive for renouncing instincts. The impetus for good behavior is fear of external authority. The possibility of severe punishment inhibits undesirable behavior. Early morality is a matter of prohibition or approval, imposed on the child from without.

A fundamental change takes place when this external authority is internalized through the establishment of a superego. "The phenomena of conscience then reach a higher stage. Actually," says Freud, "it is until now that we should speak of conscience or a sense of guilt."[2]   This stage produces the erection of an *internal* authority, and renunciation of instinct owing to fear of it, that is, fear of one's own conscience.

During the Oedipal phase, therefore, renunciation becomes a dynamic source of conscience; instead of expressing revenge, the child takes unattackable parental authority into himself by means of identification. "The authority now turns into his superego and enters into possession of all the aggressiveness which a child would have liked to excercise against it."[3]   In other words, some of a person's instinctual aggression is transformed into an inhibiting counteragency that curbs anti-social behavior. The superego's enforcement is based upon rewarding good conduct with a sense of guilt.

The internalization of aggressive instincts by parental identification has its obvious disadvantages. During the Oedipal period, the ego struggles against instinctive wishes. Out of this struggle the superego develops, aiding the ego to hold down powerful id drives. The ego becomes less independent and its enjoyment of id drives diminishes. Indeed, the ego must now mediate almost constantly between the competitive drives of the id, the demands and enticement of environment, and the moral prohibitions of the superego.

In addition to its function as a prohibitory agency, the superego punishes and rewards. Feelings of inferiority originate in disapproval by the superego. Often, this lowered self-opinion stems less from "real" reasons than from the unconscious internalization of a critical parent. But the superego that punishes an individual also rewards. When a person thinks or behaves morally, the superego rewards him with feelings of satisfaction. Thus, the superego can raise a person's self-esteem and enhance his sense of superiority.

The growing child's first identification is with his parents. As the superego develops, the child tends to inter-

nalize moral ideas similar to those of his parents. These
include attitudes toward the opposite sex, kindness toward
others, and notions of honesty. Much of the transmission
is by example, much of it comes through discussion and
reflection.

In middle childhood, in adolescence, and in adult life,
a person expands his circle of identification to include
others. Every person belongs to many groups, and a concommitant of belonging is identification with other members. The childhood gang, the adolescent clique, and the
adult special interest group are often marked by a strong,
capable leader. The members of the group identify with the
leader, whose moral standards and ideals become moral
laws for the group. The leader's superego, in a sense, becomes a part of each member's superego. This characteristic
transfer explains a part of group psychology and establishes
the responsibility of some leaders for influencing moral
thought, values, and conduct.

Summary

In the explanation of these processes, then, psychoan-
alysis gives us a theory about the ways in which culture is
assimilated and perpetuated. With the institution of conscience, a function of the superego, the individual becomes
a part of society. In this sense, the superego functions to
maintain civilization. Just as parents developed superegos
out of early relationships with a mother and father, they
in turn contribute to the establishment of superegos in their
own offspring. Although this process of transmission does
not produce identical superegos in all children, it does
produce similar superegos. The results are moral codes
shared by a society—part of the culture that constitutes each
generation's inheritance.

Child Development and Morality

Many teachers believe that thought and values fall into
wholly separate categories. At some point, the child thinks,

at some other point, he feels. One lesson deals with knowledge, another with values. The origin of this belief is obscure, for neither Freud nor Piaget promotes this dichotomy. Piaget specifically disabuses us of the notion when he writes ". . . affectivity and intelligence are indissociable and constitute the two complimentary aspects of all human behavior."[4] If this is the case, then each stage or period of Piaget's developmental theory should reveal something about affective development as well as the better known products of intellectual development.

Infancy and Emotions

Infancy begins with birth and ends somewhere between eighteen months and two years. By the end of infancy, language and thought have begun, and the child sees himself as one object in a world of external objects. During infancy both affective and intellectual development take place.

The infant clearly shows interest in his body, in his movements, and in the results of his movements. He distinguishes between the agreeable and the disagreeable, between pleasure and pain, and between success and failure connected to his own intentional acts. If a child uses an object as a tool to pull another object within reach, pleasure flows from success, and leads to his repeating the action and generalizing it to new situations.

Intellectually, the infant builds an initial sense of self and constructs the beginnings of an objective universe. Emotionally, the infant connects joy with success and sadness with failure. Next comes the imagery and language of early childhood.

Early Childhood and Moral Values

In early childhood, the child develops intuitive intelligence as he perceives events, thinks about past events, and anticipates consequences of future events. This thinking involves language: the child can talk to others, he can talk to himself, and he can create mental images and manipulate them. The child can think intuitively for himself and can engage in social relationships.

The young child's play is imitative and symbolic, a means of reliving past pleasures and solving past problems. As is the case with dreams or daydreaming, the child is changing what was real into what was desired. Until the end of this period, play is primarily solitary rather than collective. The same holds true for rules in playing. Each child tends to play both by and for himself, and the rules are his rules.

These dual rules illustrate egocentricity in social relationships. The young child does not differentiate between his own point of view and that of his playmate. If a point of view is expressed, it takes the form of an assertion. No facts or arguments are stated to support the assertion; the bold statement stands supported only by egocentricity. Logic lies beyond the child; intuition based on perception is the hallmark of this period.

Affectively, interests and values play ever stronger roles in the mental life of the young child. Interest regulates the uses of energy. A child who develops an interest in something works hard; if use brings satisfaction, then these things and activities become valued.

These interests and values become linked to feelings of adequacy or inadequacy. Success builds self-esteem and raises aspiration for the near future, but failure diminishes self-esteem and lowers aspirations.

This early system of values and early self-evaluation influences affectivity in social relationships. When people socialize, they express their values in subtle ways to see how others respond. As a child already respects his parents, what they value becomes a criterion for determining good from bad or right from wrong. The parent orders, the child obeys. Normative rules thus become part of a child's mental life.

With other adults, however, there is no inherent reason why a child must like and respect them. If a child believes an adult thinks well of him, responds favorably to his interests, or holds the same values as he does, then he tends to like that person. From this positive mutual evaluation grows respect based on affection. This sense of respect between child and adult is a source of moral feelings and moral knowledge. If the adult is respected, then what the adult values tends to become what the child values.

Whatever their source—obedience to parents, success, affection—a child does not reason out these moral ideals, nor does he justify one ideal over another when they conflict. The child accepts the idea that telling the truth is "good," even when he does not always tell the truth. The child's morals in this period are largely subject to the morals of his parents or some other respected adult.

Affectively, this period of mental development brings expansion of interests, identification of mutual interests and values, feelings of respect based on mutual evaluations, and the first moral values based on the nature of unilateral respect. The child can now move into a period marked by cooperation and reflection.

Middle Childhood

This period, known as one of concrete intelligence operations, produces the beginnings of logic and the appearance of social cooperation. The child can work or play by himself, or he can work quite effectively with another child or a group. Rather than talking past each other, children between seven and twelve talk to each other. This discussion often provides the stimuli for reflection.

The basis for these developments in cooperative and reflective behavior lies in a child's ability to distinguish between his own point of view and that of a playmate. Once he can make this distinction, the child can join with others in searching for facts to support statements. Children begin to explain objects and events to each other, and these explanations clearly show that thinking is taking place.

Cooperation requires that at least two children see each other as having equal personal value. One may be better at something, but the other also performs in some manner earning the admiration of the partner. Each child thus values the other, and this valuation leads to new forms of moral thought and feelings.

When children of this period are observed at play, rules and the following of them become important. No longer is collective play a case of each child playing by his own rules; now each child agrees on the rules and appeals to them or to an umpire in the case of a conflict.

Children of this period believe that they can make their own rules for play and that they are as good as those handed down by adults. This assumes, of course, that the children involved have agreed to the rules. Again, what comes into the situation is mutual respect. Honesty in a game is good not because adults say cheating is bad, but because cheating violates an agreement made by the members of the group. When two groups come together to play softball, there is often discussion of "ground rules" used on the home playground. Once the rules are agreed upon, they are to be followed; deceit now becomes a serious matter. If the rules are not applied consistently, the game breaks up, there is name-calling, there may be fights, and the attitude of one group toward the other becomes fixed.

Justice may be an adult term, but children have meanings for the term and they have strong feelings about these meanings. Justice involves absolute equality. Who you are makes no difference if you cheat; you must be punished the same as any other member of the group. Justice may be tempered by consideration of intent, but there must be justice if things are to set right.

Parents and teachers should understand that children in this period reflect on adult behaviors. Piaget holds that notions of justice ". . . ordinarily appear as a reaction to the adult rather than an acquisition from him."[5] The younger child submits to adult authority without thought, but during middle childhood, this authority may be seen as injust, usually due to inconsistency in punishment or to unfairness in severity of the punishment. The result of feeling and thinking about the situation leads to a separation of justice from submission to adult authority. When this happens, the child turns more and more to interpersonal relationships with friends for ideas and feelings about justice.

This new source of moral values becomes integrated with earlier values. Even more importantly, conscience no longer remains an external matter. The voice of the parent may still be heard in mental memory, but the often louder voice comes from the child's ideas and feelings. Honesty and justice are based on engaged experience with peers, and on reflection and strong feelings of reactions, rather than on compliance with the words of adults.

This period provides development of autonomous moral feelings, of a system of values combining feelings, thought, and conduct. This affective progress marches hand in hand with intellectual development. Each always affects the other and both arise from social relationships based on mutual respect and leading to discussion and reflection.

Adolescence

Somewhere after eleven or twelve puberty occurs and the child becomes an adolescent. The striking intellectual difference between childhood and adolescence is the adolescent's ability to group problems and the build theories about them. The fifth-grader tackles one problem at a time. He may generalize his solution to a subsequent, similar problem, but he seldom pulls several solutions into a general relationship or theory.

The growth of affectivity, or the confrontation of moral causes and ideas, is often on an abstract level, much the same as their concommitant intellectual theories. These causes and ideals are invested with strong emotions. Characteristically, the adolescent expresses disgust with adults who accept a discrepancy between ideal and less than ideal behavior, or who acknowledge the power of status quo interests in resisting achievement of idealized societies. Values become organized into hierarchies based on both thought and intensity of feelings. These ranking of values lead to some sort of plan for one's life. With freedom from economic want, the adolescent will cling stubbornly to his plan except as time and experience modify his metaphysics.

Disaffection with adults has a particular consequence for many adolescents. They shift their love for parents to love of some supreme being or charismatic leader. Often this leader is their own age or only slightly older, but he or she will always hold ideas seen as highly moral. This shift of affection is accompanied by the conviction that the convert will play a major role in bringing peace, justice, and brotherhood to a world badly in need of reform. Even when the adolescent does not involve himself in some project of religious, social, political, or educational salvation, he will talk about it. In his discussions, there may be arguments about solutions, but not about the need for change.

Summary

Piaget provides us with a fact-based theory of the mind in growth. He moves from the infant's construction of a practical universe into the concrete world of childhood and then into the hypothetical reconstruction of the world by the adolescent. Through each period of mental development, affectivity and intelligence complement each other. Affective development begins with egocentricity and adult authority; it moves on to mutual respect among persons and to cooperation among members of a group. Respect, cooperation, honesty, and justice develop progressively from period to period into ever more efficient means of thinking, feeling, and behaving morally.

Moral Values and the School

American psychology has produced theorists of importance, but to date none has been as influential as Freud or Piaget. We have, however, produced a mass of empirical data, giving us insights into human development and the impact of society on developmental patterns, that generally support the propositions put forward by Freud and Piaget.

Our studies on the role of rewards, for example, support the idea that the child wants love and affection from his parents. Parents, in turn, reward acceptable behavior with love and affection. In consequence, the child learns to act in ways pleasing to his parents and rewarding to him. Consistent action brings consistent rewards, so whatever is basic to those actions becomes part of a child's sense of morality. Through a system of rewards or punishments that connect ideas, actions, and feelings, the child begins to distinguish good from bad, "clean" from "dirty," right from wrong.

Early rewards are experienced in family relationships; later rewards flow from other groups as well. Regardless of the group, the individual wants to gain and maintain love, affection, and self-esteem. In these interpersonal relationships, the child identifies with someone who becomes a model. He involves himself psychologically with this model and assumes his ideas, attitudes, and conduct. He sees himself as a reflection of the other person and acts as he thinks his model does. This model-oriented behavior brings rewards from the model, from others who admire the model, and from the child's own feelings of enhancement.

Of course, each person has many potential models, but none is imitated unless there is some sort of reward. A model can be a literary or historical figure, or it can be a living person either in the immediate or distant environment. What is necessary (beyond reward) is that the child must have some knowledge or beliefs about the potential model. One further fact, often distressing to parents and teachers, is that strongly rewarded identifications are not easily changed.

Models and the School

When the attitudes and values expressed by parents and by teachers are consistent, then they are strengthened and reinforced in the child's mental life and conduct. If parents treat children with equal fairness and teachers are similarly fair with pupils, then ideas and feelings about fairness are strengthened. Furthermore, there is a tendency for such pupils to have positive attitudes toward teachers and schools.

When the attitudes and values of a family differ from those of a teacher, then the teacher's influence is diminished. The reasons are fairly obvious. First, early learnings are strong, often buried in the unconscious, and new attitudes and values do not merely fill a void—they modify or replace earlier moral learnings. Second, the teacher is an itinerant in the child's life; he wanders into the child's experience for a school year and then drops out of sight. Third, the child must return home each day to a particular and well-established climate; what has been newly learned at school dissipates easily under parental pressure. Fourth, many teachers do not consciously think about helping children acquire a sense of morality, nor do many teachers realize how or when they do affect moral values.

In terms of change, children identifying with one or both of their parents will change the least. The child seeking independence from his family, thus forging a new identity, will change the most. And, as we shall soon see, this change will more likely be influenced by the peer group than by the teacher.

Three potential sources of identification for pupils are peers, teachers (including coaches, administrators, etc.) and idealized conceptions of historical and contemporary figures encountered in their studies.

Why do children and youths form or join groups? Every reason psychologists can isolate argues for the satisfaction of some physiological or mental need. The group provides social interaction and dispels loneliness. The group works on projects of interest and eliminates boredom. The group provides sources of power, status, or prestige, and thus enhances self-esteem. The group offers relief from the pressure of grades and gives security and a sense of adequacy to those who are insecure about grades. The group provides the means of acquiring things that must be competed for—praise for humor, dates, and so forth. The group also sets standards its members can meet and it provides constant approval of behavior consistent with those standards. Joining a group leads to an awareness, directly or subtly, of that group's standards. Deviation is punished by deprivation of rewards, ridicule, rejection, or exclusion. If there is conflict between personal and group standards, the individual must change or drop out. If the individual has no clear standards for particular activities, then he accepts the group's standards. For good or for bad, the need for group life is tremendous during childhood and adolescence, and one role of a group is to enforce conformity to the extent of changing attitudes and values.

Teachers provide a second source of identification. Pupils imitate teachers, but they do not often identify with them, partly because they do not see them as models for life. It is also true that many boys do not identify with women teachers because women elementary teachers do much of the negative socializing. Of course, some pupils may take on attitudes towards learning and reasoning from teachers. They may learn to value careful experimentation and the search for facts, or they may acquire a teacher's tastes in music or art, but it is not clear that pupils generally strengthen their moral values because they choose teachers as models.

Historical figures—say Anne Sullivan in the film about Helen Keller—may generate admiration and incline a pupil to a belief, but the contact is so limited that morality is not affected much. In most cases the pupil simply does not have enough knowledge of the historical figure to identify with that figure's values. Athletes, musicians, singers, and movie stars are more likely models simply because life outside the school extols these persons. The child has more information—he can watch Joe Morgan pat a loser on the back or see how Liza Minelli acts on a television show—and knows the figure is a center of public attraction.

Other School Influences for Change

Morality arises from experience and reflection on that experience. If morality is to change, then the individual must have new experiences relevant to the desired change, he must have opportunities to discuss and reflect on these experiences, and he must receive what he perceives as rewards for considering change or changing.

A person who has prestige with students or is trusted by students will effect some change in the direction he advocates. This change, however, is maintained only when there is frequent assocation with this person and his message. The critical determinant, of course, is identification with the "communicator."

Some teachers use fear or other strong emotional appeals in an attempt to change attitudes. Interestingly, because there is some change with an emotional appeal, but almost none with strong threats of fear, which induce worry and anxiety, the pupils act to defend themselves against fear. The pupil stops listening or directs his anxiety toward the person delivering the fearful message. Or, anxiety is turned inward and the pupil focuses on it rather than the message. Research rather clearly shows that threats, dire warnings, and lurid descriptions of evil consequences have little effect on long-term attitude change.

What about the use of logical arguments presented by a teacher or by instrumental materials? Logic is not as influential as teachers would like to believe. Research does provide us with three clues about the use of logic. (1) If you know some of your pupils are opposed to what you see as a desirable value, then they are likely influenced if facts and arguments are presented for both sides of an issue. (2) If pupils are favorable to a desired value, then they are most likely influenced by positive facts and arguments. (3) The both-sides-of-the-issue procedure works best in either case with the best educated students.[6] Actually, logic is limited as a tool for two reasons: teachers tend towards one-shot treatment of moral issues, and teachers simply control the reward factors involved in a classroom discussion or lecture.

What about teachers' messages and groups? It is clear that a teacher's attack on a dominant attitude of a group has little effect on members for whom the group has value; the most likely effect is reinforcement of the group attitude and diminished status for the teacher. On the other hand, if a group has desirable values and a teacher can induce a pupil with undesirable attitudes to join the group (and the group to accept him), then change in the desired direction may well occur in that pupil. Teachers may also try to get a pupil to leave a group, but this works only when that pupil can join another group that will provide him with suitable rewards.

What about the role of personal involvement in value change? In some ways, this is the most effective tool most teachers have. Athletic coaches, for instance, are often highly successful with youngsters where classroom teachers have failed because they involve these pupils in something they want to do, which makes them susceptible to change. The young athlete involves himself intellectually, emotionally, and physically and he sees the results of his efforts (often a reward in itself) as well as receiving reinforcement from the coach.

Rather than being satisfied with the sit-still, read, recite, pass-the-written-test circumstances of too many classrooms, teachers might ask themselves the following questions: How often are class goals mutually set by students and teachers? How often do students state their own aspirations for achievement? How often do students cooperate to reach a mutual goal? How frequent are the rewards in the classroom? How often do teachers permit students to be totally involved—intellectually, emotionally, physically—in a classroom?

Research shows that the more the teacher can involve the student in, say, role-playing, the more the student is likely to take on the morality of the person who ordinarily lives the role.[7] Why? Simply because by approaching the experience of another person, he can take on that person's attitude. He is forced to consider the viewpoint of another person, and this consideration fosters change. The success of role-playing and of simulation games in elementary grades shows that significant changes can be made in attitudes through personal involvement.

Remembering facts to pass an exam brings no desirable changes because personal involvement is lacking. If students are given data and asked to draw their own conclusions, then change is possible. Teachers who require and reward reasoning and problem-solving are concommitantly requiring personal involvement, and this active participation also makes change possible.

Lastly, what is the role of teacher-student relationships? If a teacher cannot build some form of mutual esteem with a student, then desired change cannot result from teacher behaviors. Studies of parent-child relationships for aggressive boys show four facts useful for teachers: (1) early relationships lacked warmth and affection; (2) the parents controlled the boys primarily by physical means; (3) the boys showed little emotional dependence on either parent; (4) since the boys did not identify with either parent, what parents saw as desirable values were never internalized by the boys.[8] Following this line of reasoning, if ridicule, deprivation of privileges, a cold manner, or physical punishment are used by a teacher, or if the teacher shows no interest in a pupil, then the teacher is suggesting that he rejects that pupil as a person. The pupil cannot identify with such a teacher and consequently his needs cannot be met by associating with that teacher.

Summary

Teachers are entering, again, a period when questions are asked about character education and about the acquisition of morality. Teachers will attend meetings on these topics. They will read journal articles and listen to inspirational speeches during orientation week. New books will be written, new programs will be devised, new materials will be advertised. Each of these activities or events may have some desired effect, but if there is to be a substantial effect, it must come from what teachers are and do.

What will make the difference is what you, the teacher, believe, feel, and do. Will you see that each of your students gets some rewards that enhance self-esteem? Will you engage in mutual self-evaluation of interests and values with youngsters? Will you behave in ways that let students react to you in desirable ways? Will you find ways to let students make and judge some of the rules they live by in your classroom and school? Will you create situations where students can talk, freely and without fear of your ridicule, about issues of importance to them? Will you let them make mistakes and then let them reflect on them without grading them down for the original mistake? Will you seek means for learning that gives youngsters some sense of participation and utility in their society?

If you can answer yes to these questions, then your effect on their moral knowledge, values, and conduct may well be both substantial and desirable.

[1]Sigmund Freud, *Civilization and Its Discontents*, trans. James Strachey (New York: W. W. Norton & Company, 1962), p. 71.

[2]Ibid., p. 72.

[3]Ibid., p. 76.

[4]Jean Piaget, *Six Psychological Studies*, trans. Anita Tenzer (New York: Vintage Books, 1967), p. 15.

[5]Ibid., p. 57.

[6]Frederick J. McDonald, *Educational Psychology* (Belmont, California: Wadsworth Publishing Company, Inc., 1965), p. 350—52.

[7]Ibid., p. 352—55.

[8]Ibid., p. 357—60.

PART 2

TEACHING MORALITY

6

Teaching Children
with Deficient Value Systems

David A. Joseph, M. D.
Pamela B. Joseph

Larry cannot learn because he seeks to attain only immediate pleasure. Paul, too, is an academic failure and directs his energies to gaining membership in a group of defiant children. Kathy is a clever shoplifter and has few feelings about the moral consequences of her actions. Bob shows severely delinquent behavior and has built so many defenses that he cannot hear the demands of his conscience.

These four children display learning and behavior problems that a teacher may one day have in his or her classroom. Their behaviors and backgrounds are different, but one can trace their problems to a common origin: lack of moral development has interfered with their ability to learn or has influenced their delinquent behavior. Such students frustrate teachers because of their persistent behavior patterns that seem unpenetrable by the teacher's "normal" way of teaching and dealing with "normal" children.

This chapter presents studies of these four children and offers interpretations of their apparent behaviors based on their social and psychological histories. The interpretations are grounded on psychoanalytic theory, and we encourage the reader to refer to the preceding chapter on moral acquisition for an understanding of terms. We hope that these studies will lead the teacher to realize his or her own limitations in teaching students with deficient value systems as well as offering hope to the frustrated teacher that there are some ways to help these children.

Four Case Studies and Interpretations

Larry

Larry, age nine, is in the fourth grade at an inner-city school. He is not a special case; he shares, with a great number of his classmates, a short attention-span, an inability to complete assignments, and feelings of discouragement that interfere with his attempts to learn. Larry does not display delinquent behavior, but his difficulty in learning frustrates his teacher who likes this seemingly bright, personable youngster,

His teacher occasionally catches glimpses of Larry's ability when he really likes and becomes involved with a classroom activity, especially any material presented as a game. Larry learns and even retains skills and information when he is "turned on" to the activity. However, most of the time he is very impatient and cannot work through even short assignments. For example, when given a piece of construction paper for a drawing project, he starts to draw for a few seconds and then immediately crumbles up his paper. He repeats this pattern until the teacher allows him no more paper or runs out of supplies. He will not erase or try to correct what he believes are his mistakes.

His teacher once asked Larry if he thinks that getting an education will help him in life, and he told her that he knew he could get a good job someday if he got an education. Nevertheless, his non-learning pattern persists.

Larry's homelife has been unstable and certainly could be labeled underprivileged. His parents separated when Larry was an infant, and several husbands and boyfriends of his mother have lived in his home since then. His mother occasionally leaves Larry and his two sisters with her mother for several weeks at a time, and when she returns, she usually moves the family to another apartment. Larry goes to school fairly regularly, but often feels tired and hungry. He does not feel that his life will change for the better.

Larry's teacher blames his unstable homelife for his learning problem. However, in comparison with the many underprivileged children in this classroom, Larry does not manifest a severe emotional disturbance. Since he is not delinquent, the teacher does not think Larry's problem relates to his moral development.

Bruno Bettleheim considers that learning problems in children like Larry can be traced to their basic psychological framework.[1] He links the problems of these children to their deficient value systems, including underdeveloped and poorly functioning egos and superegos. Bettleheim believes that these children are underprivileged not only because of economic wants, but because of severe psychological deprivations that prohibit their chances for a better life through education.

The first thing that educators must realize when confronted with children like Larry is that schools are based upon a middle-class morality that includes the tenet that in order to gain lasting satisfactions, one must postpone immediate pleasure. Actually, those who really want to succeed might undergo hardship in order to accomplish academic success. Of course, not all middle-class children have the capacity to live according to this middle-class morality; but few lower-class or poor children can do so.

Larry cannot learn in school because he is not developing the psychological foundations necessary for operating with this middle-class morality. First, his superego is not developing, and without fear of a parent or of losing parental affection, Larry does not have enough anxiety for learning. Bettleheim believes that until children's rational powers and curiosity operate sufficiently, they need anxiety about their parents' (or, by proxy, the teacher's) disapproval in order to work and learn. As long as this fear that children experience does not overwhelm them, it serves as a persuasive motivating agent. Also, worries about losing parents' respect leads to concern for losing one's own self-respect; Larry does not respect his parents or himself.

Second, Larry's ego is not strong enough to allow him to postpone immediate gratification or see the possibility of future rewards. He is not guided by a strong reality principle so that he can do more than just intellectually acknowledge that education could help him. His mother and many adults with whom he has contact live for the here and now. He cannot internalize a strict parental superego or ego. Like the adults around him, Larry lives only by a primitive ego that is always a pleasure ego.

Larry can learn in school occasionally, but only what he wants to learn. By appealing to his pleasure principle, the teacher will give him a few dabs of knowledge here and there, but Larry will remain essentially uneducated. In fact, by making learning appeal only to Larry's desire for pleasure or emotional excitement, the teacher further thwarts his chances of ever developing a functioning ego. The teacher may capture his interest briefly, but must lead Larry to the realization that there are satisfactions to be gained in the postponement of pleasure.

However, trying to help a student strengthen his ego does not call for grim, stifling teaching methods. For example, if students such as Larry "turn on" when playing a game, the teacher first may capture their interest by playing a game, but the next day spend five minutes teaching a skill in order to improve the game-playing. Thus, students momentarily would postpone the pleasure of the game and understand why they need to learn a new skill. The teacher hopes that the students will increase their capacity for skill or knowledge-building, and eventually value the learning taking place not only to help them play a game, but for more far-reaching goals.

Of course, the obvious fact of Larry's physical deprivations cannot be overlooked. He cannot learn if he is hungry and tired, he will not believe that there is a better future to be had by postponing immediate gratification if he only knows that he must grab for what he can get now, or go without.

Paul

Paul, age twelve, is a seventh-grader at a suburban, middle-class junior high school. His teachers always have labeled him a "follower." As a young child he clung to other children and did the bidding of bullies or strong leaders in the class. Lately, Paul has gravitated toward a group of seventh- and eighth-grade boys who are known as the school "toughs." They have been involved in incidents of vandalism and have smoked cigarettes and marijuana in school. Although at first the group had no use for Paul, they allowed him token membership because of his faithful, almost puppy-like obedience to the group's leaders. To most of his teachers Paul appears passive and sulky, and often shows defiance of the teachers and rules by grumbling and responding with painful deliberation.

Paul's performance in academic areas often is pitiful because he often knows the material studied and demonstrates his knowledge in discussion, before or after an examination. On tests he usually answers a few questions, leaves most of the paper blank, and sometimes scribbles over it. On an I. Q. test two years earlier he demonstrated above-average intelligence.

Paul developed an unusually friendly relationship with his language arts teacher during this school year and achieved above-average grades on several examinations. On one test, he received the highest grade in the class. His teacher praised him before his classmates and later reiterated her praise to him privately, suggesting that he show the test to his parents. He answered, "My mother only cares when I do bad."

Paul is quite accident-prone and blames his frequent minor injuries and poor school work on bad luck. He shows no confidence in himself and speaks disparagingly of his own abilities.

Paul's family background seems stable, at least on the surface. He has four siblings, lives in a comfortable three-bedroom house, appears well-dressed and well-fed. Both parents work in order to afford this suburban life-style. The parents' main concern is for bettering their financial position and acquiring possessions. There appears to be little closeness in the family and the parents limit their role to that of caretakers. The family never participates in activities together, such as religious or community organizations. The children have responsibilities for maintaining the household, and are forbidden to join any extracurricular activities at school or in the neighborhood.

From the brief sketch of Paul's family and school history, it is obvious that his moral behavior hinges on many factors besides the development of his conscience. The little voice warning of moral misdeeds (assuming some conscience has developed) becomes overpowered by other strong messages: "I am powerless and alone, I feel inferior; I need to belong." A clinical diagnosis could describe Paul as a masochistic personality—authoritarian in the sense that he has a compulsive need to conform to his peers.

Paul's isolation stems from his homelife, which is sterile and unwarm. The way to get some personal attention from his parents, he feels, is to do poorly in school in order to elicit some form of concern from them, or, more specifically, from his mother. The predominant values he observes in his parents are desires for material success. Other values do not come through clearly. His parents have not communicated a system of beliefs, and other community agencies, except the school, were not given the chance to give their messages. The school communicates "work hard, do well," but success in school is not appreciated in Paul's home; it is matter-of-factly expected. The parents have contributed to Paul's paralysis of initative and self-confidence. His home has not filled the void of his loneliness.

The feeling of powerlessness and loneliness lead Paul to deprecate himself and conform without limits to his peers. Paul fits Erich Fromm's description of a masochistic authoritarian character:

> masochism as aiming at dissolving oneself in an overwhelming strong power and participating in its strengths and glory. Both the sadistic and masochistic trends are caused by the inability of the isolated individual to stand alone and his need for a symbiotic relationship that overcomes this aloneness.[2]

The accidents, failure in school, and belief in his bad luck demonstrate Paul's masochistic tendencies and his feelings of powerlessness.

Paul has not experienced adult authority as warm or supporting. He often feels defiant towards adults who represent his parents, and yet he does not defy the authority of his peer group. It fulfills a need for him to belong, and so he blindly follows strong peers, even if they represent delinquent values. Indeed, those who strongly defy adult authority seem very attractive to him. Defiance of adult authority is an attempt to overcome his feelings of powerlessness. He seeks power in his attachment to the group, and allows the group or group's leaders to determine his values, to function as his parents. While rebelling against adult authority, he manifests childlike dependence on the group.

Kathy

Kathy is a fifteen-year-old high school sophomore. She is pretty but not too popular. Her friendships last only a short time. The only people who stick by her are some of the more delinquent people in her class. Kathy's school work is average to below average and there are times when she has trouble concentrating in class. It is during these times that she starts to talk louder in class. Her behavior becomes very giggly and flighty. She stops doing her homework assignments. It is only with a very strong concerted effort of the teacher that Kathy begins to do her work again.

Occassionally, Kathy does not show up in class for days at a time. She completes some of her work, but the majority of it remains unfinished. Her teachers begin to feel frustrated and angry with Kathy because they have put in a great deal of effort in trying to help her, but as soon as attention is focused away from her, she gets into more difficulties. Her teachers usually lose interest or give up trying to help because they cannot meet Kathy's need for constant supervision.

Upon further investigation one could see where some difficulties might arise. Kathy was adopted by her family at age one and a half. She has a younger brother who was adopted from the same agency four years later. She grew up in a middle-class neighborhood. When she was ten years old her parents were divorced. They gave up the house in the middle-class neighborhood and the children moved with their mother to an urban area, where Kathy is currently going to high school.

Kathy's adoptive father was in business. He had wanted to be a lawyer and had finished law school, but failed the bar exam five times. The reason the family adopted the children was that after seven years of marriage they found out the father was sterile. Since the divorce, Kathy's father was convicted of income tax evasion and has been on parole. Kathy has not seen him in the last few years. She feels he is not interested in her and that he never really cared about her.

Kathy's mother is very aloof and really interested only in herself. Constantly accusing her daughter of not telling the truth, the mother feels Kathy is a con artist and will do anything to get her own way. Kathy and her mother are very much alike.

Kathy's mother always seemed to come home with some new appliance or item of clothing. Kathy did not know where all of these things came from as her mother earned so little money. It was not until she herself began shoplifting that she figured things out. Kathy found that she could steal almost anything, right in front of the salespeople in one of the largest department stores in town. One day she walked out with nine overcoats, one at a time. She gave the clothes away to her delinquent friends who could not organize themselves to steal as well as Kathy.

Kathy is aware of what society judges as right and wrong and usually is able to make socially acceptable choices. Her ego functions adequately and can keep most of her impulses under control. This can be seen best by her relative lack of sexual experience within a group that is notorious for its promiscuity. However, a decision of doing something one way or the other makes no difference to her. She has no anxiety about an act that would get her into trouble and no guilt once she has done it.

In school she needs to be reminded by her teacher about the consequences that would befall her if she does not get her work completed. If she does not do her work, she feels no guilt. Only when confronted by the teacher is she contrite. Once the contact with the teacher ends, there are no longer any guilt feelings. Hence the accusation by her mother that Kathy is a good actress. However, she is not acting when the teacher confronts her; she feels genuinely guilty. But she cannot maintain an internalized superego: she needs a real one in order to experience guilt or anxiety about her actions. The teacher's presence is needed in an authoritarian capacity to create the anxiety that is necessary for Kathy to learn.

The focus of Kathy's case has been on a superego deficiency. This does not mean that there is no superego at all. She may have the rudiments of one, but it is based on the behavior of her parents and is defective. The superego may function well in some circumscribed area but break down in other areas.

Bob

Bob, a fifteen-year-old in the ninth grade, is frequently absent from the classroom. When he shows up, the teacher usually wishes he had not because Bob is loud and boistrous. He reacts to the teacher's attempts at discipline with an escalation of his disruptive behavior. Finally, the teacher exercises the last possible alternative: he removes Bob from the class.

The teacher invariably hears a number of excuses when he tries to talk with Bob. "He did it first!" (Accusing another student of initiating the same behavior.) "We were all in it together." (In other words, why just pick on me? Everybody else was disruptive too.) "I had to do it or I would have lost face." (One of Bob's friends had accused him of being "too chicken" to talk back to the teacher. This friend had done this in a previous class. Now it was Bob's turn.) Bob then apologizes profusely for having been so disruptive.

Bob has a long history of delinquent acts going back to a runaway incident at age eight. He has been picked up ten times for shoplifting, twice for stealing watches out of dormitory rooms at a local college, and four times for beating up some enemies from a nearby town.

Bob comes from a lower middle-class background. His father lost his job because of alcoholism. His mother also is an alcoholic. Bob has a deprived homelife because of the family's precarious finances and violence stemming from terrible fights between his parents. The fighting often drives Bob from home. Because he has no close relatives or siblings to turn to for comfort or guidance, Bob became involved with a gang of boys as a substitute family. Under pressure from the gang, he began his history of criminal acts and arrests.

Children who manifest behavior like Bob's may be from different family constellations or situations. Whether parents are overburdened by just trying to survive or are putting all their energies into amassing a fortune, the net result is the same: the child is left to grow up on his own. No one frustrates, modifies, or sublimates his impulses. The family does not help him build an ego or superego through love or fear; they abandon him to the impulses of his id by their neglect. Lack of parental interest in his development is the most important factor in understanding Bob's delinquency. Bob and Larry are both deprived children, but attention from his mother and the extended family gave Larry enough input to develop a rudimentary value-system.

Bob uses various means of justifying his behavior and in doing so protects himself from experiencing guilt. His ego is deficient in controlling his impulses and he has, as Redl and Wineman say, a "delinquent ego."[3] In the delinquent ego, every energy is geared to the defense of impulse gratification. Instead of looking for a way to synthesize desires, the demands of reality, and the impact of social values, the ego is momentarily on the side of impulsiveness. What the ego does is try to help justify what is happening to the superego, thus avoiding the experience of guilt. In this way, id impulses can be fully gratified without any worry about guilt.

The ego abandons itself to the id and an alliance is formed with the id to gratify all desires. A healthy ego would be able to delay and modify the discharge of the impulses and desires until such a time that the discharge would not produce much anxiety. However, the delinquent ego is not capable of delaying or modifying for very long because it is overwhelmed by the impulses and the intensity of the desires. There is a push for action that is not modified by reality testing.

Rudiments of a superego are present, albeit in a more punitive, harsh form. This can be seen with Bob in his overly apologetic manner in his talk with his teacher. He feels guilt, but it is too late and too intense for the behavior he exhibited. The ego fails to hide the reality of his behavior

when subjected to the confrontation by his teacher. If
allowed to go without confrontation, Bob would have successfully eluded feeling any guilt. The guilt is only momentary and Bob does not learn anything from the experience.
The guilt is not connected to the behavior: witness his ten
arrests for shoplifting. He is unable to modify his actions on
the basis of his experience and the ego function of reality
testing is deficient. Bob does not feel any anxiety about
being caught while shoplifting; the thought hardly enters his
head. But, when he does get caught and is confronted over
and over again with his behavior, he experiences overwhelming guilt.

Bob is a very difficult person to deal with effectively. He
has had few adult figures with whom he could identify, and
even those are fleeting. He will not let anyone come into
contact with him in order to help. One must disrupt the
pattern of gratification that he has evolved over a period of
time and only after this is done can Bob be reachable and
teachable. To change means to give up the id gratification
and to come more into contact with reality.

Interpretations for Teachers

Bob's case is on the extreme end of the spectrum,
although "normal" children occasionally manifest similar
problems. The progression from functioning primarily on the
pleasure principle to functioning on the reality principle
occurs gradually. Once children gain this capacity, living by
the reality principle is subject to regression and temporary
disruption in the face of anxiety, intense instinctual wishes,
or developmental crises or conflicts. Such setbacks in
children's developmental patterns are different from breakdowns of reality testing that occur in adult forms of
psychopathology.

Teachers confront an almost limitless array of behavior
each year. The precise meanings of each behavior cannot be
appreciated until one uses the historical perspective in order

to gain understanding. Two children can exhibit similar behaviors, but their actions may mean different things.

We have tried to illustrate, by use of these case studies, abnormalities that occur in the development of moral behavior. The four cases suggest some general principles and guidelines for educators: (1) In order to teach children and adolescents, their basic needs must be met. (2) If children suffer because they lack food, they cannot learn. (3) If they live in fear of beatings at home or experience turmoil because of emotional crises at home, such as divorce or death, the chance of learning taking place is slim.

However, children's inner needs often remain neglected. These needs also demand satisfaction in order for learning to take place. Normal children, to a large degree, begin schooling with many needs unfulfilled. The traditional time for formal education occurs about the time of latency, which is the period between the resolution of the Oedipus complex, at age five or six, and the onset of puberty. It marks a relatively calm period in the child's inner life in which the pleasure principle is put under some semblance of control and the reality principle dominates. The child reinforces the dominance of the reality principle by identifying with his parents, taking on their prohibitions and attitudes.

According to Bettleheim, only through modifying the pleasure principle can learning take place:

> Lacking a very strong superego we can still learn, on the basis of our emotions, what for one reason or another we want to learn, but we can learn only that. Such learning can and does take place on the basis of the pleasure principle. That is why educators who try to reach their students this way are amazed at how fast and how much their children learn. It is also why they quit in disappointment when everything breaks down as soon as learning can no longer proceed on the basis of the pleasure principle only. All other learning (which means most of it) can occur only when we have learned to function on the basis of the reality, because learning that

gives no immediate pleasure satisfaction requires that we function by the reality principle, that is, we are well able to accept displeasure at the moment, and for some time to come, in the hope of gaining greater satisfactions at a much later time.[4]

Larry is an example of how a child, both internally and externally deprived, functions in the classroom on the basis of the pleasure principle. Teachers who have students like him must realize that making school enjoyable is important, but not the most important thing for such children. Ego strengths also must be built. We cannot stress enough the need for the teacher to assess the student "where he is at" and adjust teaching methods to maximize learning. However, we again assert that helping children to postpone gratification does not mean obliterating pleasurable classroom activities. In teaching children with deficient value-systems, the educator also must realize other internal needs of the students. Building a child's self-confidence—making him feel good about himself—goes hand in hand with building ego strengths.

Paul's case is different because he could learn in school. However, his poor school performance reflects the only way in which he gets attention at home. The consistent friendly support of the teacher provides Paul with one of the first opportunities to experience pleasure and attention for his positive performance. The breakthrough that the language arts teacher encouraged suggests that future positive, supportive relationships with adults might decrease Paul's defiance of adults and his compulsive conformity to peers.

Kathy's case demonstrates the effect of a superego deficit. One can trace her delinquent behavior and poor school performance to the negative-role models of her parents. Only through intense and persistent attention given Kathy did the teacher modify her behavior in school, but, of course, once attention decreases Kathy fails to respond. Kathy needs the teacher to function as a superego for her, but realistically, what teacher can give her such immense amounts of constant attention? But she must have such relationships with adults in order to learn or function morally. In this case, the teacher and therapist must work together to help Kathy.

Bob has a severe ego deficit. He still functions on the basis of the pleasure principle, and as in Larry's case, only by appealing to the pleasure principle can the teacher promote some learning. But, unlike Larry, Bob displays severely disruptive behavior when he gets no immediate gratification. Only in a complete treatment setting will Bob be able to get the help to check the demands of his impulses and begin to function on the basis of the reality principle.

All of these children present difficult problems to teachers, but only through understanding their needs and deficits can teachers help them to learn. Teaching styles, methods, and approaches to relationships with children must be modified to fit student's individual needs—a difficult and demanding task, even if we taught only one child each day. Through an understanding of the mechanisms or deprivations that create poor learners and behavior problems, the task may seem possible and will, we hope, become less frustrating.

[1] Bruno Bettleheim, "Moral Education," in *Moral Education/ Five Lectures*, ed. Nancy F. Sizer and Theodore R. Sizer (Cambridge, Mass.: Harvard University Press, 1970).

[2] Erich Fromm, *Escape from Freedom* (New York: Avon Books, 1966), p. 246.

[3] Fritz Redl and David Wineman, *Children Who Hate: The Disorganization and Breakdown of Behavior Controls* (New York: Macmillan Co., 1951), pp. 169—229.

[4] Bettleheim, *op. cit.*, pp. 95—96.

7

Values Clarification:
A Critical Perspective

Bruce D. Johnson
Bryce Nelson

The values clarification movement is a popularized effort
to promote a form of affective education through the use of
value-laden teaching strategies. The teaching approach
usually consists of small-group exercises which emphasize
learning a process through which value decisions may be
made. The format might best be described as value education, as opposed to moral education, as it deals only marginally with moral values. In spite of some criticism for not
dealing more substantially with questions of morality,
values clarification has received considerable attention from
teachers and teacher educators. For that reason, the values
clarification strategies and philosophy merit a careful examination.

If large sales of values clarification books and high attendance at values clarification workshops are indications of
success, then the values clarification movement must be
judged a successful effort at values education. The strategies,
created as an attempt to bring self-awareness to students,
have been adopted by many concerned teachers who have
perceived a need to bring values instruction into the classroom. Values clarification has met this need by offering
well—organized, highly imaginative, pertinent materials for
classroom use. As the most visible of several efforts at value

education (See Chapter 3), values clarification must be given credit for providing a possible methodology for classroom consideration of individual value choices.

The ensuing examination of values clarification is in three parts. First, a brief summary of the historical context of the movement is presented, indicating connections to the Progressive education movement and to the more recent humanistic education movement. A second section explains and in part criticizes the values clarification procedures. It serves to caution teachers against using the strategies without first attempting to totally understand the potential effects the procedures might have upon students.

The third section concerns implications values clarification strategies have for the classroom setting and for the role of the teacher. In using values clarification it is essential to understand the classroom dynamics involved. Anyone contemplating their use should, if possible, attend one of the workshops offered by values clarification leaders to discover the suggested classroom approach. One is also advised to read as much of the material as possible, including the rationale stated in *Values and Teaching*.[1] The teacher, as portrayed by the values clarification materials, becomes in effect a moderator or facilitator of a socializing activity, guiding students through a process designed to help them individually order their alleged value confusion. This process may be successful for some, but by emphasizing process instead of content the teacher may be de-emphasizing cognitive growth for other students. Is it better to teach a process for learning how to develop an attitude or value, or is it better to teach some of the traditional moral principals upon which our culture and society are based? The answer to this question affects pedagogy. The authors of *Values and Teaching* phrase their answer clearly: ". . . most of us became teachers because we wanted to teach somebody something. Most of us are all too ready to sell our intellectual wares. The clarifying strategy requires a different orientation; not that of adding to the child's ideas but rather one of stimulating him to clarify the ideas he already has."[2]   Thus, the teacher should be aware of the teaching role required by the material and feel comfortable about playing that role.

Historical Context

Professor Louis Raths and Sidney Simon, Raths's doctoral student in curriculum at New York University, developed values clarification in the late 1950s. Raths had been heavily affected by Dewey's *Theory of Valuation*[3] and *Moral Principles in Education*,[4] and by Robert Lynd's *Knowledge for What?*[5]   Simon had been strongly influenced in the direction of Dewey's ideas while teaching in New York's progressive Lincoln School between 1954 and 1957. Merrill Harmin, a fellow graduate student of Simon's, became interested in their work and has remained an important figure in the values clarification movement.

At the time values clarification was created, the educational climate was not ready for its acceptance. Because of ideological competition with the Soviet Union, prominent voices called upon public schools to provide a stronger academic curriculm for all students, with emphasis on mathematics and the pure sciences. Progressive educators were considered responsible for the perceived academic decline in public schools.   One form of progressive education, the Life Adjustment movement, was a visible example to critics of this anti-intellectual drift.   Life Adjustment was an attempt to give useful, practical help to adolescents who were not benefitting from an academic curriculum, and who were about to leave public schools and begin finding their place in society.   Critics of Life Adjustment said it was undemocratic and not in the national interest to give an inferior academic education to a large segment of the school population, while giving other students a rigorous academic education aimed at achieving excellence.   Thus, a clash existed throughout much of the 1950s between proponents of the two schools of thought.

Values clarification received little attention until the mid—1960s, when the educational mood had shifted, and an academic education for all no longer seemed practical or desirable. *Values and Teaching,* published in 1966, is still the fundamental explanation of values clarification. Basically, Raths contributed the theoretical parts, while Simon and Harmin collaborated with him on the text and also wrote the exercises. In the late 1960s, Howard Kirschenbaum, Simon's doctoral student at Temple University, emerged as another important figure in the movement. Kirschenbaum's interest in group dynamics and the client-centered group therapy of Carl Rogers helped bring these two emphases into the movement. The publication of other values clarification literature has been largely a post-1972 phenomenon. The themes of many of the exercises in these materials remind us of the internal divisiveness the United States experienced during the late 1960s and early 1970s. Clearly, the implementation of values education meant that public schools were attempting to meet needs quite different from those considered important during the height of the Cold War.

A mood of moral questioning pervaded the United States for a decade from the mid-1960s. It was prompted by the political emergence of racial minorities, the war in Indochina, the Watergate scandal, and spurred on by the youth movement. Few institutions escaped the scrutiny and questioning of critics and dissenting reformers. Rhetoric espousing the values of various movements was heard from street corners to classrooms to pulpits. When current events create crucial questions, such questions most certainly have a place in the classroom. These events ostensibly helped prepare the climate so that educators became receptive to material like values clarification. But educators talked about values clarification for reasons other than those prompted by political events, and for purposes other than civic education.

The recent interest in values education in public schools is only partly related to the political crises and public immorality of the past decade. Values clarification has become popular in part because it clearly is a component of the humanistic-oriented movement designed to remake public education.   As one variation on the legacy of progressive education, values clarification originators have tried to tie classroom activities to the "needs of the child." This has taken the form of confronting students with the need to think about their value choices in their immediate lives, and at the same time to feel positive about being in school and about the people around them.   Simon described values clarification as " . . . one of a number of individually directed psychological and sociological theories that also embrace re-evaluation counseling and what has become known as Encounter or Interaction Groups."[6]

The nature of this humanistic movement implied dealing with student behavior problems with therapeutic techniques. Within the social and political context described above, and the concommitant attack from both sides of the ideological spectrum against public schools thought to be inept and oppressive, many educators have been receptive to humanistic goals—especially if the behavior in school of troublesome students could be improved.   Implicit in the 1950s criticism of the Life Adjustment progressives was a question that still nags public schools and that is basic to assessing the place of values clarification: How can schools promote academic excellence and at the same time not abandon those students who are not benefiting from a rigorous academic curriculum? As we shall see, values clarification seems to have not been designed to promote rigorous moral education, but to focus instead on the less academic, humanistic side of this dilemma.

Values Clarification Procedures

Values clarification books are essentially handbooks of teaching strategies.[7]   To gain an understanding of the procedure they use, an examination will be made of the rationale behind the movement, followed by some examples of values clarification strategies. The strategies, too, will be critically evaluated, as will a series of assumptions upon which values clarification theories are based.

Rationale

John Dewey pointed out that teachers would be indignant at the accusation that moral instruction was not being undertaken in the classroom.[8]   Moral education, he contended, was a natural part of their daily work. Although values clarification is only partially interested in moral questions, this observation of Dewey's nevertheless seems to have become peripheral for the rationale behind values clarification. Today, much of the rationale for it is based upon a perceived absence of value training in the schools.

From Raths's early writings on values clarification through the most recent publications, the rationale has been to improve behavior of troubled (not mentally ill) young people.[9] Operating upon the theory that behavior problems are related less to emotional disturbances and low I. Q.s and more to a lack of clear values, the clarification writers have postulated that this material could help the student to see what values were being held, how they conflicted, and how they could be clarified. A person whose values needed clarifying exhibited apathy, listlessness, flightiness, uncertainty, inconsistency, drifting, overconformity, overdissention, and role playing. They observed "troubled students" as not yet having found a "meaningful role for their lives and therefore unable or unwilliing to marshall up their full intellectual resources for use in the crucial game of living."[10]   Through values clarification they were to become proud of themselves, cognizant of their new-found values, and " . . . behave in ways that are less apathetic, confused, and irrational and in ways that are more positive, purposeful and enthusiastic."[11] We must note, however, that the moral element in some value questions ought to make some students angry at injustice,

despondent over prospects for change, or righteously indignant with people around them. That probably would not
lead to "positive, purposeful and enthusiastic" behavior.

One of the premises upon which the precedures are based
suggests that traditional educational, cultural, and religious
institutions no longer adequately prepare people to select
personal values and to live by them. "Everyone," asserts
Simon, "is for values. The problem is that they have become
meaningless."[12] Values clarification looks back to a simpler
Golden Age where values were transferred by moralizing,
" . . . the direct, although sometimes subtle, inculcation of
the adults' values upon the young."[13] Various traditional
ways in which this was accomplished are no longer thought
to be successful. Simon thinks educators are interested in his
material because " . . . they look and see how many peoples'
lives are adrift and are full of apathy and listlessness . . . I
think that teachers are finding kids harder and harder to
teach, harder to keep interested and harder to feel involved
with."[14] Values clarification advocates assume that the
breakdown of the family unit, proliferation of mass media,
and geographical mobility have made far too many choices
available, thereby making it harder for a young person to
to make any choice at all. (This overlooks the fact that any
choice may be hard because there are only a few worthy
options.)

The existence of conflicting viewpoints means to clarification proponents that organized religious, ethnic, or other
community groups would not allow public schools to promote a particular value system.[15] Hence, values clarification
concentrates on the process for making a value decision
rather than the content of conflicting value positions. The
authors summarize:

Too often schools supply only a knowledge of facts, concepts, or cognitive skills. Yet this knowledge is not
enough to equip people for coping with problems in to-

day's pluralistic and complex society. Young people have
become aware that their schools are failing them and an
increasing number of students are no longer willing to
tolerate a curriculum that does not acknowledge their
needs, interests and concerns. Schools, as well as homes,
must offer young people a way to develop a set of values
upon which they can act and base their lives.[16]

The Process

In *Values and Teaching,* the authors define values: "Out
of experience may come certain general guides to behavior.
These guides tend to give direction to life and may be called
values. Our values show what we tend to do with our limited
time and energy."[17] A value, they suggest, is not viable until
it has undergone the seven-step series of sub-processes based
upon choosing, prizing, and acting. Those steps are: (1)
choosing freely, (2) choosing from alternatives, (3)
choosing after thoughtful consideration of consequences,
(4) prizing or cherishing the value, (5) publicly affirming it,
(6) acting upon it, and (7) acting upon it regularly. "Unless
something satisfies all seven criteria," the book suggests,
"we do not call it a value."[18]

The seven steps to a value attempt to make a value choice
something that is personally important to the individual
making the choice. A choice made without all steps is a value
indicator. Value indicators hint at what the individual
prefers, such as goals, aspirations, attitudes, interests, feelings, beliefs, activities, and worries. Through the exercises,
value indicators are to be elevated and become values.

Critics of values clarification strategies have attacked the
notion of having to take "steps" in order for an individual to
possess a value. Alan Lockwood, for example, observed that
to make a distinction between values and value indicators is
"needlessly arbitrary." He further argued that the insistence
upon "regularly performed criteria for a value . . . fails to
deal with the problem of determining what action(s) is
entailed by possessing a value.[19]

Requiring arbitrary choices between values and value indicators creates some problems. First, an individual may fulfill the required procedure and truly value something, even if the value is potentially menacing to society or to himself. Second, the procedure ignores the fact that certain values or moral principles grow out of a cultural context, as is explained in Chapters Two and Three. Third, the procedural insistence upon regularly performed criteria seems to overemphasize the process of making the decision over the content of the decision. For example, the Values Continuum Strategy poses the question, "What should the U. S. attitude be on involvement with other countries?"[20] The student is to select an answer from the following continuum: "Help every country even if not asked to do so . . . or, help no country—complete isolation." The question could be the basis for a lengthy seminar, yet strategies suggest going quickly to the next question, one that concerns an individual's popularity in a group. By over-stressing a process, the system may be precluding the necessity of learning the content of moral principles upon which a value should be based. If carefully and thoroughly implemented, values clarification could be helpful in leading some students to an understanding of larger moral principles, but the exercises do not encourage that sort of care and intellectual work.

One of the schematic approaches set forth in *Values Clarification*, entitled "Either-Or Forced Choice," proposes a situation that is traumatic at worst, and meaningless at best. Questions such as "Are you more of a loner or a grouper? More like breakfast or dinner? More like a 'No Trespassing Sign' or a 'Public Fishing' sign?" etc. force a person to determine a self-concept.[21] Such examples remind us that the authors commonly use open-ended terms, and that the student is expected to supply most of the meaning for these exercises.

Another approach is to select a "value" from a continuum of choices. For example, a teenager would be given the following question: "Which do you think is the worst?

_____to become (or get someone) pregnant (unwed)
_____to be dependant on hard drugs
_____to date someone from another race."[22]

In such a case, the student is requested to make a choice between possibilities that may or may not be applicable. The exercise may produce a satisfactory answer for some students. For others, the peer pressure or sense of coercion may provoke students to respond with sentiments they do not really possess.[23] Difficult moral decisions seem to be difficult in part because the context of the situation does not allow the person caught in the dilemma to think rationally and apply a principle or method. How, then, is one to respond publicly to an exercise that has for its context the anticipated reaction of one's fellow classmates and teacher?

A game called "Life Inventory" raises an additional issue. Sample questions include: "What things do you do well? Are there some values you are struggling with? Tell about one missed opportunity in your life. Was there a time of heavy grief? More than one?"[24] Questions such as these point to the sensitive, highly personal nature of some strategies of values clarification, whose proponents presume that students are willing to share deeply personal information and beliefs with peers and with a non-threatening teacher. Few students will fail to cooperate in the presence of a skilled teacher, but one is forced to wonder about the ethics of such a methodolgy. If, for example, a student does not wish to comply, even though the teacher has assured him that he need not feel compelled to respond, may that student be jeopardizing his standing with the teacher? There should be a point beyond which the teacher ought not to encourage or expect personal information from students.

Some exercises in *Values and Teaching* ask for personal data that is probably no longer available to the teacher due to recent legislation, court cases , and school district guidelines dealing with the student's right to privacy and access to confidential school records. Further, if values clarification is dealing with "psychological education," it is imperative for the teacher to understand the ramifications of the questions. Is the teacher really willing to be involved with the emotional adjustment of many students over an extended period of time? Can the teacher be a value-free moderator of discussions? Is the teacher competent to heal when wounds are opened? And is this role going to be supported by other faculty, administration, parents, and community public opinion? Kohlberg observed about the psychological aspect of values clarification:

> I think they deal with a much broader field than moral values or moral development. Values cover everything under the sun. A lot of what they call values clarification is what other people call psychological education. They talk about feelings, needs, and desires as equivalent to values. When you do that, you get into interesting aspects of psychological education that we don't want to deal with.[25]

Assumptions

Several basic assumptions have been prominent through the two-decade existence of value clarification. The first is that people lack values or are unclear about those they possess, as exhibited through the behavior characteristics described earlier. But, as shown in Chapter 5, many social scientists believe that although values are not always articulated, they are nevertheless present—learned through a process that involves the influence of home, peer-group pressures, reactions to experiences, and institutional training.

Second, it is assumed that most students are basically rational and want to clarify, consciously and purposefully, their values and improve their behavior. Simon notes: "The process of clarifying our values and giving meaning to our lives is a deeply rational one, never whimsical. It is in the most significant sense an intellectual process . . . "[26] With

progressive educators of other decades they share a creed
built on faith and optimism in people: ". . . if we can recognize, accept, and express our own feelings we can consider
alternatives and consequences and make our own choices,
and if we can actualize our beliefs and goals with repeated
and consistent action, our decisions will lead us toward a
future we can cope with and control."[27]   Teachers considering using values clarification ought to consider whether or
not they are comfortable with this.   Clarification authors
grant that some students will not be interested, but this
seems to be dismissed as a minor problem.

The third assumption is that practice in making values
choices on structured exercises will actually lead to a rational
clarification of personal values, and that such values will be
applied in real-life situations. There is no distinction drawn
between practice in making value decisions and practice in
making moral decisions. The assumption is that the moral
nature of a dilemma will be self-evident, and that making a
choice for moral reasons is not fundamentally different from
making any value choice.

Fourth, the values clarification materials assume that
there are ". . . no absolute right or wrong answers for
another's values questions."[28]   While such an assumption
leaves room for sensitivity to a student's beliefs, it also
implies an "anything goes" ethic. The authors do not consider themselves to be moral relativists, yet because their
exercises deal only marginally with moral principles, the
thrust of the material is in the direction of relativism.

Fifth, it is assumed that the teaching of a form for values
selection will aid the socialization process of learning how to
function in this society.

Sixth, there is the assumption that the age of the student
is not very important for values to be successfully clarified.
It is hard to tell for what age group an exercise is intended
although most exercises seem to require high school knowledge and maturity. Presumably, teachers are to use whatever material seems right for their students. Developmental

psychologists such as Kohlberg argue that people go through stages of moral development, and hence are ready for certain pedagogical approaches, classroom climates, and subject matter only at certain times in their lives.[29]   The values clarification authors do not explicitly take this developmental approach, although they have acknowledged Kohlberg's influence. Occasionally they give separate lists of questions that seem appropriate to different age groups rather than to different levels of moral judgement.

Classroom Implications

An analysis of values clarification would be incomplete without a consideration of the classroom dynamics involved in the approach. In so doing, it is worth remembering that the movement has changed since to late 1950s. As teachers pick and choose exercises from the clarification books, they should be aware of these evolutionary shifts and recognize how these changes were designed to meet a specific need at a particular moment. That mood and that need may have passed now, and consequently the exercise may no longer be as useful as it once was.

The Group Process

Many values clarification strategies are dependent upon group processes and group dynamics for implementation and, thus, may create some unusual teaching situations. Authors of the strategies advise the teacher to create a classroom climate of trust and acceptance, where students are encouraged to enjoy being a part of a group. In most teaching situations this is, of course, desirable. However, when dealing with value choices and, in some cases, with moral dilemmas, the possibility exists that peer pressure to accept group values will result. The teacher must remain sensitive to the complex problems involved with group situations.

By advocating group procedures, the values clarification movement has moved increasingly toward an emphasis upon verbal rather than written exercises, thereby giving little time for reflection and usually no time for background preparation. Unlike *Values and Teaching*, the more recent literature on the subject rarely introduces the exercise, gives a day or so for thought and study, and finishes later. Instead, a brief explanation precedes the exercise, thereby increasing the likelihood of facile talk using ill-defined general categories, undue influence by one or two individuals, and the forced necessity of immediate decisions. It is hard, in such a situation, to keep group discussion to a point and to clearly spell out concepts. In *Values and Teaching*, the authors recognized the problem: "One does not get values in the busyness of a classroom discussion, especially a heated discussion. One needs quiet, hard thought and careful decisions if one is to have clear, persistent and viable values. These do not easily come in the midst of a room full of talking."[30]

The Teacher Role

The relationship between teacher and student is vital in order for valuing to work, as discussed in Chapter 5, and hence it is important that the relationship not be broken. More recent values clarification literature, however, takes a very non-directive approach, suggesting that young people do not need or want the guidance of adults. This attitude would seem to jeopardize the teacher-student relationship. *Values and Teaching* proposed that the teacher was to clearly set limits for acceptable behavior options before the student made a value choice: "If for many reasons we don't want him to choose a particular alternative, like setting fire to the house, we should let him know that this is not within the realm of choice. We should not try to fool him into thinking that he is a free agent and then disappoint him when we refuse to honor his choice."[31] Six years later, Simon noted, interestingly, that teachers who needed to limit their students' options should not use values clarification: "Teachers who think their students are too young and inexperienced to have developed worthwhile ideas should not use the approach. Values imposition would probably be more their style; and they should be open about it and not hide behind values clarification jargon and techniques."[32] Simon thought that teachers who failed with values clarification did so because they were teaching incorrectly, rather than because of any inherent problems with the material: "I'm really overjoyed that in the hands of a crummy teacher it comes out crummy work, and students just don't do it anymore."[33]

For Raths and Simon, valuing could only have meaning for a student when concerns important to him were the objects of the valuing process. Students would see through a teacher's attempts to guide their answers in a direction desired by the teacher and thus would quit thinking and working on the valuing process. In *Values and Teaching*, they say:

> If the teacher—no matter how subtly—were to make judgments or provide standards in a values clarification discussion, he would be depriving students of the privilege of making their own decisions about the topic under consideration. Moreover, he would be implying that students cannot do their own thinking and their own valuing, an implication that, if frequently repeated, would tend to convince students that it is so. The result would be the conformity, apathy, indecisiveness, and overdissenting of which we spoke earlier. Value confusion, in short, cannot be cleared by a process of clever teacher direction.[34]

The teacher helping students clarify their values is not only not to indoctrinate them with his own views, but is not even subtly to guide students toward desired positions with

leading questions. "Don't moralize, no matter how subtly
...It is contrary to the theory," they say. [35]The teacher must
let the students thrash around ideas in a completely free, open
environment. Simon claims the result of moralizing for the
student is that ". . . too often the important choices in life
are made on the basis of peer pressure, unthinking submission
to authority, or the power of propaganda."[36] His own
method hardly seems free of these. For most exercises, the
teacher is to reveal his position at an appropriate ending in
the discussion, or at least reveal his choices. Speaking about
the teacher's role, Simon and Clark say that "if we are not
prepared to let others know what we value, values clarification will be considered just another pedantic farce."[37]

There are several problems with assuming that a relatively value-free classroom can be made in order to clarify
values: (1) The peer-group pressure and the verbal nature of
the exercises create value images and influence decision-
making. (2) The responses to the exercises will be affected
by biases implicit in these exercises. (3) Students bring a
more or less developed sense of valuing to the classroom, and
hence, when they substantially raise the value concerns, they
may deal disproportionately with peripheral concerns.
(4) The teacher's revelation of his own values tends to affect
the group. And (5) the teacher has an obligation to point
out the overriding importance of questions of social justice
and not to imply that all moral and value options are of equal
importance.

Responses to the exercises will be affected by the biases
and assumptions that come through the exercises. Simon, for
example, wants to see a student who is not very materialistic,
an individual rather than a conformist, and one who "feels
free."[38]

The preference of the teacher would necessarily become
evident to the students over a period of weeks. At the conclusion of a discussion, the teacher's sharing of personal
values would give clues to a class, and possibly inhibit future

discussion.   If the teacher expressed doubt and confusion about too many things, students might look elsewhere for guidance. Clearly a teacher's views are heard in an *ad hominem* manner.   However, in *Values and Teaching*, the authors indicate that a teacher with unclear values would pose no problem: ". . . a teacher who can operate in the style of this value theory can help children, and we see no reason why teachers with less than clear values cannot do this. The crux of the issue is whether or not the teacher can control his behavior enough to give his students what they need or would like to give them."[39] Such dispassion seems quite difficult to achieve.

By being primarily concerned with methodology and secondarily with content on value questions, is a teacher abdicating a legitimate role in shaping values? It is probably not the place of the public school teacher to advocate a position on equivocal issues such as pre-marital sex, abortion, euthanasia, or land-use policy, but it is teacher's place to make sure that the implications of decisions on topics like these are understood. In *Values and Teaching*, the authors affirmed that the teacher ". . . may be authoritative in those areas that deal with truth and falsity. In areas involving aspirations, purposes, attitudes, interests, beliefs, etc. we may raise questions, but we cannot 'lay down the law' about what a child's values should be."[40] Should the teacher have such a dispassionate attitude toward social injustice, racism, and denial of fundamental rights? Or do we argue that the innate reasonableness of students will enable them to see the ideal values by themselves? In values clarification the teacher is not to be an advocate for the traditional ideals of social justice, but rather just a dispassionate facilitator of student ideas.

A teacher can be interested in moral education that is not classroom indoctrination and be quite sympathetic toward affective education, but still have the foregoing reservations about this particular brand of curricular material.

Summary

Values clarification is a pedagogical technique designed to teach students how to go about making value decisions for themselves. The material deals only secondarily with specifically moral questions. Affective goals of changing the behavior and self-image of students are more important than the content and correctness of the value decisions made on the exercises. Shifts have occured in the movement since the late 1950s, so that in material published since the early 1970s various affective learning techniques have become more prominent. The movement is a part of the larger, humanistic effort to remake public education, and as such presents a sharp option to the more traditional cognitive approaches. There has been a need by many educators for curricular material aimed at the values and self-image of students. The available material adequately serves some purposes, but questions remain concerning its educational usefulness.

[1]Louis Raths, et. al., *Values and Teaching* (Columbus, Ohio: Charles E. Merrill Publishing Co., 1966).

[2]Ibid., p. 54.

[3]John Dewey, *Theory of Valuation* (Chicago: The University of Chicago Press, 1939).

[4]John Dewey, *Moral Principles in Education* (Carbondale, Ill.: Southern Illinois Press, 1909).

[5]Robert Lynd, *Knowledge for What?* (Princeton: Princeton University Press, 1939).

[6]Sidney Simon, *Meeting Yourself Halfway* (Niles, Ill.: Argus Communication, 1974), p. xiii.

[7]Values clarification books include: Louis Raths, Merrill Harmin, Sidney Simon, *Values and Teaching* (Columbus, Ohio: Charles Merrill Publishing Co., 1966); Sidney Simon, Leland W. Howe, and Howard Kirschenbaum, *Values Clarification* (New York: Hart Publishing Co., 1972); Merrill Harmin, Howard Kirchenbaum, Sidney Simon, *Clarifying Values Through Subject Matter* (Minneapolis: Winston Press, 1973); Sidney Simon, Robert C. Hawley, and David Britton, *Composition for Personal Growth* (New York: Hart Publishing Co., 1973); Sidney Simon, *Meeting Yourself Halfway* (Niles, Ill.: Argus Communications, 1974); Sidney Simon and Jay Clark, *Beginning Values Clarification* (San Diego: Pennant Press, 1975); Sidney Simon, *I Am Loveable and Capable* (Niles, Ill.: Argus Communications, 1974).

[8]Dewey, *Moral Principles in Education*, p. 3.

[9]Sidney Simon and Jay Clark, *Beginning Values Clarification* (San Diego: Pennant Press, 1975), p. 62, and Raths, et al., *Values and Teaching*, p. 182.

[10]Raths, et al., *op. cit.*, p. 7.

[11]Ibid., p. 11.

[12]Simon, *Meeting Youself Halfway*, p. x.

[13]Simon, et al., *Values Clarification*, p. 15.

[14]Simon and Clark, *Beginning Values Clarification*, p. 22.

[15]Sidney Simon and Howard Kirschenbaum, *Readings in Values Clarification* (Minneapolis: Winston Press), p. 17, and Raths, et al., *op. cit.*, p. 18.

[16]Merrill Harmin, Howard Kirschenbaum, and Sidney Simon, *Clarifying Values Through Subject Matter*, p. 17, and Raths, et al., *op. cit.*, p. 18.

[17]Raths, et al., *op. cit.*, p. 27.

[18]Ibid., p. 28.

[19]Alan L. Lockwood, "A Critical View of Values Clarification," *Teachers College Record* 77 (1975): 37.

[20]Simon, et. al., *Values Clarification*, p. 116.

[21]Ibid., p. 94.

[22]Ibid., p. 81.

[23]John Stewart, "Clarifying Values Clarification," *Phil Delta Kappan* 51:10 (1975): 684.

[24]Simon, et al., *Values Clarification*, p. 316.

[25]Simon and Kirschenbaum, "An Exchange of Opinion Between Kohlberg and Simon," *Readings in Values Clarification*, p. 63.

[26]Simon, *Meeting Yourself Halway*, p. 14.

[27]Simon and Kirschenbaum, *Readings in Values Clarification, p. 30.*

[28]Simon, *Meeting Yourself Halfway*, p. xvii.

[29]Lawrence Kohlberg, "The Child As Moral Philosopher" in *Readings in Values Clarification*, p. 62.

[30]Raths, et al., op. cit., p. 106.

[31]Ibid., p. 34.

[32]Simon, et al., *Values Clarification*, p. 26.

[33]Simon and Clark, *Beginning Values Clarification*, p. 28.

[34]Raths, et al., *op. cit.*, p. 113.

[35]Ibid., p. 109.

[36]Simon, et al., *Values Clarification*, p. 16.

[37]Simon and Clark, *Beginning Values Clarification*, p. 46.

[38]Ibid., pp. 17, 91, 124–26.

[39]Raths, et al., *op. cit.*, p. 92.

[40]Ibid., p. 37.

8

Value Conflict:
The Teacher's Dilemma

Pamela Joseph

While introducing a unit on racism to her eighth-grade American history class a teacher experiences acute discomfort when a boy blurts out, 'Who wants to talk about those niggers, anyway?'' The teacher's confusion and anger increase because she fears that the majority of the class probably agrees with the boy. She suddenly realizes that her values conflict with those of her students. She cannot decide how to handle the student's remark and feels that teaching the unit is an impossible task. Overcome by her anxiety, the teacher cannot deal effectively with the situation.

Is the reaction of the teacher in that experience unique? Probably not; yet few educators consider how value conflicts affect the teacher. The way students deal with their ambivalent or conflicting values concerns many teachers, but seldom does anyone wonder about what happens to the teacher.

With today's emphasis on value clarification for students, teachers are portrayed as well-adjusted, unprejudiced individuals who calmly and objectively help clarify students' values. Yet, teachers, too, experience inner conflicts, feel ambiguity about their own values and face conflicts with the values of others. Such value conflicts produce many emotional consequences. Teachers feel anxiety, confusion or anger because of them, and these feelings subtly or overtly influence their dealings with students, parents, peers, and administrators.

No one can prevent value conflicts from emotionally affecting teachers, but the emotions themselves are not the real difficulties. Unrecognized or unresolved feelings interfere with effective teaching by clouding teachers' perceptions of their relationships with others, by creating so much discomfort that teachers have trouble relating to certain students or issues, or by producing so much anxiety that teachers become totally incapacitated.

Why Value Conflicts Produce Emotional Repercussions

Recognition of a problem must be the first step towards solving it, but many teachers do not believe that value conflicts cause problems for them. Their denial of anxiety (probably the most common emotion experienced because of conflict) may stem from defense mechanisms or from misunderstanding of the term value. When teachers feel no anxiety, they may not have experienced value conflict.

When people say values, they often really mean attitudes. An attitude is a preference, and thus when an attitude conflict occurs, it may cause little or no anxiety. One usually can tolerate the notion that other people have different tastes in music, or that they prefer another living style. However, some people *value* some things in a moral sense, and not just prefer them as personal choices, and they often cannot imagine how any situation could affect their beliefs.

The argument that value conflicts provoke anxiety follows this logic: If one establishes the criterion that a value is something that would make the world a better place if everyone held or respected it, and acted consistently because of it (in other words, a moral judgment as described in Chapter 1) those who do not hold the value would make the world worse and thus be harmful. Conflicting moral values then exist as threats to one's well-being, even though the threat is minimal.

For example, Joe and George have been friends since high school. They have mutual friends, similar hobbies, and belong to the same church. But Joe, a veteran, disagrees with George's belief in pacifism. Joe admires George's courage to withstand criticism about his refusal to fight, but George's views actually make Joe feel uneasy. Joe may respect his friend's courage of his convictions, but he does not share pacifism as a value. He feels that pacifism would be dangerous in case of national emergency. Conversely, George likes and respects Joe, but fears people like Joe are steering the world toward destruction. In order to remain friends, both have to ignore the issues in contention as much as possible.

Conflict does not always involve external conflict (with others). It can be internal as well. "The moral struggle goes on within people and not only between them," writes Gunnar Myrdal. "As people's valuations are conflicting, behavior normally becomes a moral compromise." He explains that "behind human behavior there are a mesh of struggling inclinations, interests, and ideas. . . ."[1]

Furthermore, he stresses that internal conflicts often remain unconscious but still influence behavior:

> The whole "sphere of valuations"—by which we mean the entire aggregate of a person's numerous and conflicting valuations, as well as their expressions in thought, speech, and behavior—is thus never present in conscious apperception. Some parts of it may even be constantly suppressed from awareness. But it would be a gross mistake to believe that valuations temporarily kept in the shadow of subjective inattention—and the deeper-seated psychic inclinations and loyalties represented by them—are permanently silenced. Most of them rise to consciousness now and then as the focus of apperception changes in reaction to the flow of experiences and impulses. Even when submerged, they are not without influence on actual behavior.[2]

Most inner value conflicts, because they remain unconscious, may be more threatening, produce more anxiety, and affect behavior to a greater extent than external conflicts.

The process of self-examination can create more confusion or anxiety. For example, when a teacher comes into a community in which the students' values appear different from his own, his anxiety can be excruciating because of self-doubt, rather than because of the obvious conflict.

The conflicts that create anxiety may be quite subtle. Even when a class is so young that controversial issues seldom are raised, anxiety is acute because basic, more primitive tensions within the teacher are aroused. The teacher then has to deal with unresolved conflicts stemming from his or her own childhood. The teacher who has not defined a personal set of values as an adult, still unquestioningly sharing his parents' moral beliefs, may overreact when a student challenges a personal value; the student provokes a strong emotional reaction in the teacher because the teacher links cherishing the value with obedience to the parents.

How Value Conflicts Affect Teacher Behavior

Because of anxiety and other emotional effects of value conflict, teachers may deal poorly with their own prejudices, judge students inappropriately, and in general reduce their teaching effectiveness. Teaching behavior resulting from anxiety varies from sophisticated rationales to avoid value conflicts to uncontrolled emotional outbursts. Most teachers react in a manner somewhere between the two extremes: they express little overt anxiety, but, nonetheless, let their anxieties control them.

One needs to look at the general effect of anxiety on individuals:

> In addition to the motor and visceral effects of anxiety, the important effects on thinking, perception, and learning should not be overlooked. . . . Anxiety tends to produce confusion and distortions of perception, not only of time and space but of people and the meaning of events. These distortions can interfere with learning by lowering concentration, reducing recall, and decreasing ability to relate one item with another (association).[3]

Obviously, teacher effectiveness diminishes when anxiety takes hold and affects the teacher's relationships with students, their families, or school personnel. Anxiety can be a serious handicap for the teacher:

> An important aspect of emotional thinking, including anxious or fearful thinking, is its selectivity. Under the influence of anxiety, a person is apt to select certain items in his environment and overlook others, all in the direction either of falsely proving that he was justified in considering the situation frightening and in responding accordingly, or, conversely, of seeking reasons for false self-reassurance that his anxiety was misplaced and unnecessary.
>
> Selective perception and thinking may affect not only the inclusion and the exclusion of events, people, and things, but also the meaning of words and actions. It may thus become an instrumental factor in prejudice, which, a priori, determines the meaning of an event before it happens or stereotypically assigns a person or action to a certain class or group on the basis of a shared attribute, often irrelevant to the action that is the focus of attention.[4]

"While there is anxiety in the lives of all of us, we build defenses to see anxiety as something that affects others, not ourselves," comments one educator.[5] Teachers are masters of this defense, and it is easy for them to focus on the problems of children when their job is to judge and evaluate others, not themselves.

Other teacher defenses include: treating emotional issues intellectually, "diluting the personal meaning of what is threatening" by making the subject impersonal and mechanical, and by giving busy work. When a teacher tries to ignore anxiety and hide his feelings from students by "acting like a teacher," the teacher creates more anxiety for everyone.[6] If the teacher who encountered negative reactions from her class at the beginning of the racism unit tries to ignore her own anxiety and teach just the "facts," she probably could not teach the unit effectively; racism is not a "cut-and-dried" subject, but an emotional topic. It would be impossible to ignore the class's feelings.

Another defense applies specifically to the teacher who declares, "I've never had any anxious moments resulting from value conflicts!" Although the teacher may be saying that he felt no anxiety over attitude conflicts, he also could be guilty of "naive cultural and ethical relativism." Anthropologist and psychoanalyst George Devereux calls this the " 'museum of customs' conception of mankind".[7]

One can imagine this defense operating in the classroom: A teacher in a ghetto school rationalizes that all attitudes and behavior are part of the students' culture and cannot be modified. He might accept antagonistic attitudes toward the school as an irrevocable cultural phenomenon, and would develop unrealistically low expectations of the students' potential for academic achievement. By rationalizing that lack of desire for achievement is an unchangeable value, this teacher blames only the students for their failure to learn.

These professional defenses require some amount of intellectualizing to achieve, but other emotional reactions to value conflict are in rougher form. Teachers can behave in the same patterns as do non-professionals, including their students.

Many teachers deal with anxiety, confusion, or anger by avoiding the source of their uncomfortable feelings. They resist contact with anxiety-provoking persons and ideas, or value conflicts that create anxiety. A sixth-grade teacher relates, "Several times I have felt that I could not deal honestly with questions concerning the legality of drugs without telling my personal opinion. My ideas probably would have conflicted with the mores of the community, so I had to hold my tongue." Similarly another teacher writes, "when I worked in a community that had quite different values than I did, I avoided issues that would make me feel uncomfortable."[8]

Reaction to anxiety also produces overt behavior. For example, Rokeach reports a "high correlation between dogmatism and anxiety."[9]   Anxious teachers may try to force their values on students by becoming increasingly dogmatic. When teachers cannot handle their anxiety, they cannot tolerate any disagreement with their belief-system.

A teacher convinced of his moral superiority might find it difficult to use value clarification techniques that demand "a psychologically safe classroom . . . in which children feel free to hold values that are different from those of other children or of the teacher." In order to use value clarification techniques, Ringness makes the following suggestion:

> The teacher is expected to feel and show genuine respect for the pupil and his views. The classroom atmosphere is nonthreatening, and trust is built up between teacher and child. Not only must the teacher be genuine in his communications with the child, he must be willing to listen to the child. The child who shows attitudes deviant from those of the teacher is not to be coerced, and is personally accepted as much as the child whose values are in line with those of the teacher.[10]

Even when teachers do not appear blatantly to force their values upon students, teachers influence students unintentionally or unconsciously. For instance, "school marks are based partly on the willingness of the child to conform to the teacher's expectations. But if pleasing the teacher is important for getting good marks, we must realize that we are evaluating not only learning, but conformity."[11]

Also, in light of recent literature about sex-role stereotyping, we know that teachers' expectations of qualities demonstrated by each sex perpetuate sex roles.[12] This process of perpetuating sex roles is similar to the "museum of customs" defense: If teachers believe girls should not be aggressive competitors, they will rationalize to themselves or the students, "Don't worry, girls aren't supposed to be successful in this subject (or activity)." Such teachers may judge boys harshly for failure to show aggression because aggression is valued in males.

A teacher may react in anger "when he is in conflict with himself and has not perceived his own anxiety," writes an educator.[13]   During a casual discussion at lunch with colleagues, a teacher who grew up in an orphanage and worked his way through school furiously attacks the welfare system and programs to help black students enter college. His emotional outburst appears to stem from his feelings of resentment, not from objective analysis. How could this history teacher teach a unit on poverty or minority groups if he could not deal with his emotional reactions to these topics?

When teachers experience acute anxiety because of value conflicts, the effect on their teaching and self-esteem can be disastrous.   Because they cannot resolve conflict, teachers often become paralyzed. The teacher who became so upset when her students did not want to study "niggers," clearly experienced frustration and a sense of failure when she could not cope with the problem.

Unresolved internal value conflicts also can paralyze teachers. For example, because a teacher cannot choose between wanting to meet the principal's expectations and carrying out a punishment in his classroom, he "loses face" before his class and lowers his own self-respect. Similarly, a teacher is ineffective because she could not take decisive action in handling an "unmanageable" child; her inaction "was largely dictated by her fear of making a mistake, her fear of social censure in the situation (by students or peers), and by her underlying rage when she felt she could not handle the problem."[14]

Problems of teacher indecisiveness or role conflict often belong in the category of value conflict. As human beings, teachers may value many things, but their fear of taking action often stems from not thinking through their beliefs and goals and defending a hierarchy of values. When one chooses between two values, the decision is neither clear-cut nor easy to make, but without choosing, the teacher can do nothing but suffer the uncomfortable consequences.

Dealing With Anxiety

How should we deal with teacher anxiety generated by internal or external value conflict? We cannot train teachers who can treat value conflicts and yet not develop anxiety. If one really cherishes a value, one will experience some anxiety when someone holds another value. Instead, educators should ask, "How can we become aware of anxiety, minimize it, and use it as a constructive guide for better teaching?"

There are several steps that the teacher and teacher-training institutions should take in dealing with the problem of teachers' emotional reactions to value conflicts:

Effective teacher training

Teachers should be aware of the problem of reactions to value conflicts even before they step into a classroom. The prospective teacher "must become aware of his self-oriented feelings and attitudes and be increasingly able to cope with them." Counseling and introduction of anxiety-producing situations in seminars are two methods to help new teachers analyze their values and attitudes.[15] Of course, even without official programs or classes, one hopes that the future teacher would try to prepare himself for anxious situations. Also, new teachers could profit from demonstrating materials on controversial topics to each other in order to understand their own values on these subjects. However, anticipation of anxious situations is no guarantee that anxiety will not occur when a teacher handles a conflict in reality.

Understanding the values and problems of others would also help new teachers cope with conflicts in their classrooms, schools, and communities. For instance, knowledge of the special problems of adolescence is needed by middle-school and high-school teachers since adolescents themselves often are in turmoil because of painful value conflicts that occur when they become critical of parental values and seek their own beliefs and standards. Also, teacher-training institutions should encourage the individual prospective teacher to obtain skills, experience, and positive attitudes to be used in dealing with the many minority, economic, age, and social groups which he is likely to encounter.

Observation of behavior

It is not enough to ask teachers to take value tests. On paper, teachers may affirm whatever they like; in class, their behavior reveals actual values. Holt points to the inconsistency between the values teachers and administrators affirm and the values they demonstrate. He feels that even though teachers may say they like and respect children and their individual differences, they are really saying ". . . if I tell you that you are wise, but treat you like a dangerous criminal, you will feel what I feel much more strongly than if I said it directly."[16] Teachers may think they are conducting democratic classes and tolerating conflicting values of their students, but in reality their obvious displeasure or anxiety could create a stifling atmosphere in which students feel the need to conform or just react negatively to the teacher, materials, and school itself.

Prospective, and experienced, teachers need to observe their own behavior in the classroom. Video or audio taping of class sessions reviewed by the teacher is an effective method. For the courageous, peer evaluations for signs of anxiety or dogmatism could be undertaken. Furthermore, awareness of how students behave and feel in both open and stifling environments leads to more sensitive teaching. Interviews can also help teachers gain empathy with their students.

Self-awareness

When teachers talk about educational psychology, they refer to their *students'* behavior and personalities. When they discuss values they usually refer to *students'* values. Moreover, many teachers perceive their roles as static, forgetting that they—as human beings—change, grow, or act inconsistently. Awareness of students' reactions, therefore, does not provide the whole picture of classroom dynamics. Because teachers' behaviors influence their relationships with students and affect the learning process itself, teachers must know themselves—their attitudes, beliefs, prejudices, and the complexity of their emotions. Notwithstanding the cautious arguments raised in Chapter 7, work by pre- and in-service teachers in values clarification seems one logical prescription for understanding one's own values.

Reading about values, emotions, and classroom dynamics that emphasize teachers' behavior and feelings would give insight to teachers about the problems caused by value conflicts. The following readings are recommended:

Anthony, James, "The Reaction of Adults to Adolescents and Their Behavior," *Adolescence: Psychosocial Perspectives*, ed. G. Caplan and S. Lebovici. New York: Basic Books, 1969.; Devereux, George, *From Anxiety to Method in the Behavioral Sciences*. New York: Moulton, 1967.; Fromm, Erich, *Man for Himself: An Inquiry into the Psychology of Ethics*. Greenwich, Conn: Fawcett, 1947; Ginott, Haim, *Between Teacher and Child*. New York: Macmillan, 1974.; Moustakas, Clark, *The Authentic Teacher: Sensitivity and Awareness in the Classroom*. Cambridge, Mass.: Howard A. Doyle, 1966.; Redl, Fritz, *When We Deal With Children: Selected Writings*. New York: The Free Press, 1966. Ringness, Thomas A., *The Affective Domain in Education*. Boston: Little, Brown, 1975. Sarason, Seymour B., et al., *Psychology in Community Settings*. New York: John Wiley & Sons, 1966.

Using Anxiety for growth

A teacher from a racially integrated school commented recently, "After five years I intellectually understand the cultural differences between some of my students and myself, but I'm not sure I emotionally understand them."[17] This teacher realizes that when a conflict occurs, he cannot operate on a purely intellectual level. When this teacher feels anxiety, he does not have to hide it by being defensive. Instead, he can analyze how his emotions affect his classroom.

Rather than viewing their emotions as overwhelming obstacles, teachers should depend on uncomfortable feelings to warn them that something, perhaps an explicit or implicit value conflict, is disturbing their teaching. They can then discover the source of their anxiety, work through inner confusion or understand how an external conflict affects their performance, and reduce anxiety through comprehension of it. The dilemma caused by the failure to understand and deal with emotional ramifications of value conflicts does not have to exist. By understanding the nature of the conflicts and their emotional effects, teachers can learn to use emotions to the benefit of their students, the school, and themselves. However, awareness of one's anxiety, understanding of the effects of value conflicts upon others, and constructive use of anxiety cannot solve all the teacher's problems about values. Sensitivity to value conflicts will not resolve the teacher's moral dilemma: whether to use knowledge of value conflicts to try to attain a more ethically neutral classroom or to seek ways to change students' values.

The introductory example about the paralysis reaction of a teacher beginning a racism unit points out that even when a teacher recognizes a conflict and controls anxiety, she must take action. Several alternatives open to that teacher include: (1) thanking the student who made the remark for the honest expression of his feelings and proceeding with the unit; (2) stating that racial slurs are repugnant to the teacher;

(3) explaining that racial slurs will not be tolerated in the classroom; (4) immediately exploring with students why people use derogatory racial terms; (5) ignoring the remark at the time, but introducing material to show the roots of prejudice; (6) ignoring the remark, but later helping students empathize with groups who suffer discrimination; (7) ignoring the comment, teaching the unit, but later expressing hope that her students will not be bigots.

The alternative that the teacher chooses depends upon her feelings about self-disclosure, methods of teaching, and the teacher's right to influence student values. Educators may argue hotly about the course of action in such value-charged situations, but unless the teacher can calmly consider the alternatives—the educational and moral choices that must be made—no action is possible at all.

[1] Gunnar Myrdal, "American Values and American Behavior: A Dilemma," *Democracy, Pluralism, and the Social Studies—Readings and Commentary*, ed. James P. Shaver and Harold Berlak, (Boston: Houghton Mifflin, 1968), p. 88.

[2] Ibid., pp. 93—94.

[3] Harold L. Lief, M. D., "Anxiety Reaction," *Comprehensive Textbook of Psychiatry*, ed. Alfred M. Freedman, M. D., and Harold I. Kaplan, M. D. (Baltimore: Williams and Wilkins, 1967), p. 859.

[4] Ibid., pp. 859—60.

[5] Arthur T. Jersild, *When Teachers Face Themselves*, (New York: Bureau of Publications, Teachers College, Columbia University, 1955), p. 8.

[6] Ibid., pp. 50—51; also Owen A. Hagen, *Changing World/Changing Teachers* (Palisades, Calif.: Goodyear, 1973), pp. 81, 90.

[7]George Devereux, *From Anxiety to Method in the Behavioral Sciences* (New York: Moulton, 1967), pp. 86, 87.

[8]Data from questionnaires and interviews conducted with teachers in graduate programs at Northwestern University, May, 1974.

[9]Milton Rokeach, *The Open and Closed Mind* (New York: Basic Books, 1960), pp. 364—65.

[10]Thomas A. Ringness, *The Affective Domain in Education* (Boston: Little, Brown, 1975), p. 145.

[11]Ibid., pp. 145—46.

[12]Patrick C. Lee and Nancy B. Gropper, "Sex Role Culture and Educational Experience," *Harvard Educational Review* 44:3 (August, 1974): 369—410.

[13]Jersild, *op. cit.*, p. 45.

[14]Frederick J. McDonald, *Educational Psychology*, 2nd ed. (Belmont, Calif.: Wadsworth, 1965), p. 571; Seymour B. Sarason, et al., *Psychology in Community Settings: Clinical Educational, Vocational, Social Aspects* (New York: John Wiley & Sons, 1966), p. 104.

[15]B. Orthanel Smith, Saul B. Cohen, and Arthur Pearl, *Teachers for the Real World* (Washington, D. C.: American Association of Colleges for Teacher Education, 1969), pp. 84, 90; Dale L. Brubaker, *The Teacher as a Decision-Maker* (Dubuque, Iowa: William C. Brown, 1970), preface.

[16]John Holt, *What Do I Do Monday?* (New York: Dell Publishing Co., 1970), p. 53.

[17]Data from teacher interviews, Northwestern University.

9

Transactional Analysis: A Framework for Ethical Decision - Making

Francis Ulschak
John Nicholas

The exam is over. The test results are in. However, the teacher is not satisfied. Tom, a very good student, was in to see her and explained how he "froze up" on the exam. A grade from this course means the difference between college entry or not. The teacher is experiencing a dilemma. On the one hand, she feels that all students should be treated equally. If she makes an exception with Tom, she will not be treating the students all fairly. On the other hand, she likes to view each person as an individual and feels that individual needs should be considered. Tom may know the material and, for various reasons, may have simply messed up the exam. The test could be at fault for not reflecting his knowledge. What decision should be made? The dilemma is that two values of the teacher are in conflict. One value relates to treating all the students equally and the other value relates to responding to individual needs and situations.

This example reflects an "ethical decision." For the purpose of this discussion, an ethical decision is defined as one involving two internally held values that are in conflict. In the example above, equal treatment (all students should be treated equally) and individuality (individual needs and situations should be taken into account) are the values composing the ethical decision.

The teacher in a classroom may be involved in many types of value conflicts and ethical decisions. Our purposes with this discussion are to help the teacher and the student to understand their values and ethical dilemmas more clearly, and to offer a specific tool, contracting, as a means of resolving ethical decisions. (Contracting provides the individual confronted with an ethical decision with guidelines for moving from dilemma to problem solving.) Transactional analysis is presented as a model that teachers and students may find useful in dealing with their own ethical dilemmas as well as interpersonal ethical conflicts.

We believe that teachers' and students' ability to move from conflict to problem solving is vital not only for immediate settings but also as a model. The teacher is modeling behavior; if students are aware of the teacher's ability to deal constructively and creatively with ethical dilemmas, then they have a model of how they, too, can handle ethical dilemmas.

In this discussion we will look at four things: first, general concepts of transactional analysis; second, the interrelationship of transactional analysis and ethics; third, contracting as a specific tool that may be used in solving an ethical dilemma; fourth, exercise designed as an aid to the classroom teacher in teaching ethical decision making.

Transactional Analysis: What is it?

Transactional analysis has its origins in the writings and work of Eric Berne, who orginally developed it as a method of psychotherapy.[1]

Transactional analysis is a useful model for assisting the individual to understand: (a) his own behavior, attitudes and feelings, (structural analysis), (b) what takes place in communications between people (transactional analysis), (c) ulterior messages and covert messages that lead to misunderstanding and "bad feelings" payoffs (game analysis), and (d) unsatisfactory decisions that an individual makes about himself and the environment that affect his self perceptions and interactions with others (life scripts).

Thus, transactional analysis is a model that provides guidelines for analyzing and understanding various levels of interpersonal and intrapersonal relations. With the emphasis on analysis and understanding comes another emphasis of "getting on with," or problem solving. Along with understanding the individual is encouraged to act. In the following discussion, the emphasis will be on the individual personality, or structural analysis as it is called in transactional analysis.

The basic concept of transactional analysis is the concept of ego state. Ego state is defined as "the way in which we see ourselves and others".[2] Thus, it involves a set of perceptions about ourselves and/or the world. With the different perceptions come different attitudes and actions. More completely, ego state is said to be a set of assumptions that result in certain behaviors, attitudes, and feelings toward self and others.

Three ego states are identified in transactional analysis: Parent, Adult, and Child. (Note: In this discussion when parent is capitalized, it will refer to the Parent ego state, and when it is not capitalized it will refer to biological parents. The same is true with Adult and Child.) The standard transactional analysis diagram is shown in Figure 1. The structure diagram should not be viewed as a hierarchy, that is, showing that the Parent is more important than Adult and Adult more important than Child. All three ego states are of equal importance and value.

Figure 1.
EGO STRUCTURE DIAGRAM

P   Parent Ego State

A   Adult Ego State

C   Child Ego State

The Parent ego state contains attitudes and behaviors that the individual incorporates from external sources. These are learned and imitated decisions. The Parent ego state may have a critical and controlling view of the world, for example, "you should never do that . . .", and/or a nurturing and supportive view of the world, as, "here, let me help you with that . . ." Of great importance are the perceptions that the individual has of himself and the world. If these perceptions are critical and judgmental, then the individual is Critical Parent (CP). If they are supportive and nurturing, the individual is Nurturing Parent (NP). Both are aspects of the Parent ego state. (Note: Critical Parent may also be referred to as Controlling Parent or Disciplining Parent, and Nurturing Parent may be referred to as Supporting Parent.) The Parent ego state contains the "shoulds," "oughts," and "musts" of the individual. If a person "should always do . . .", this is a good indication of a Parent ego state message. Also, unqualified words such as "never" and "always" are tip-offs to the Parent ego state. The teacher or student operating from that state will be operating out of "shoulds" ("this is the way it should be done") and "alwayses," ("I've always done it this way") without much consideration to the present situation.

The Adult ego state is the individual's reality testing ability at a particular time. The individual is involved in collecting and analyzing data and problem solving. The Adult ego state function is often compared to a computer—simply taking information in, processing it, and giving information output. The Adult ego state uses words like "probable," "maybe," "possibility," and so on. Instead of the all-encompassing statements of the Parent, the Adult makes qualified statements. The teacher operating from the Adult will be making statements like "Frequently, I find this a useful way to do things" or "Of the various possibilities available, I pick this one." The Adult is involved in checking out reality in the here and now.

The Child ego state contains the impulses and feelings that come naturally to a child. In this state, the individual acts and feels child-like regardless of his age. The Child is composed of behaviors and attitudes that are Adapted and Free. In Adapted Child behavior, the person is continually reacting to an internal or external perceived Parent. This reaction may take the form of compliance ("What can I do to please?") or rebellion ("What ever you want, I'll do the opposite—I'll get you . . ."). Free Child, also referred to as Natural Child, is the expression of feelings that the individual is experiencing without the reactive quality. These may be feelings of anger, sadness, joy, happiness, inadequacy, confusion, etc. Significant qualities of the Free Child are the elements of creativity and energy. Since the Free Child is not caught up in reaction, energy for creativity is available. Words frequently associated with the Child ego state include "wow," "neat," "exciting," etc., and are expressive of feelings that a child might use. The teacher in the Child ego state will be responding to students with statements like "Wow! That's neat," or "Yecch! That's terrible."

Figure 2 is descriptive diagram of PAC (Parent, Adult, Child).

Figure 2.
DESCRIPTIVE DIAGRAM OF PAC

Critical Parent	CP NP	Nurturing Parent
	A	Adult
Adapted Child	AC FC	Free Child

Transactional analysis theory states that all people have a Parent ego state, Adult ego state, and Child ego state. Thus, a teacher in a classroom may be Parent, Adult, and Child at different moments in the day. And, since ego states may change rapidly, within a short period of time, the teacher may exhibit Parent behavior, Adult behavior, or

Child behavior. Students in a classroom setting will also be functioning in the three ego states. At times, they will experience themselves as Child, ("What can I do to please the teacher" or "Whatever that teacher says, I will disagree with . . . "), Adult (gathering information and decision making), and Parent ("That person always asks ridiculous questions.").

We believe that all three ego states are important for teachers and students. At times, it is very appropriate for them to be Parent, either critical and judgmental or nurturing; at other times, Adult is appropriate, and at still other times, Child. The key thing is for the teacher and student to use their ability to shift from ego state to ego state according to what is important and appropriate at a specific time.

Transactional Analysis and Ethics

Using the concept from H. D. Aiken [3] of four levels of moral discourse, it is possible for an analysis of moral valuations to be performed within the transactional analysis model just described. According to Aiken, the four levels of discourse can be distinguished as (1) "expressive-evocative." (2) "moral," (3) "ethical " and (4) "post-ethical."

Figure 3.
LEVELS OF MORAL DISCOURSE

Post-Ethical

Ethical

Moral

Expressive-Evocative

The levels are distinguished by the different purposes that the same valuational terms perform when used at each of the levels. Because of these different purposes, there are different kinds of arguments, exceptions, and "good reasons" appropriate at each level. Any moral statement that proceeds at any length is likely to shift among levels, with the shifts being functional rather than deductive in nature. Using valuational terms to perform different purposes at each of the four levels is achieved differentially through behavior originating in the Parent, Adult, or Child ego state.

Valuational Language

At the first level, valuational terms are used unreflectively as an expression of likes and dislikes. They do not solicit a reply nor call for defense; they are merely an expression of feeling. At the expressive level, then, we have behavior orginating in the Child ego state, and particularly in the Free Child, which behaves impulsively, untrained, and expressively. An example of a valuational statement from this ego state is "Wow! What a fantastic day!"

The Adapted Child might also be a source of valuational expression at this level, with expressions arising in response to traumas, experience, training, or to demands from figures of authority, an example being: "I'll never do very well in that class. It's just too hard!"

In addition to merely expressing feelings or venting emotions, valuational language is used to express or encourage empathy, or to promote values. This behavior originates in the Parent ego state. A statement such as, "Be good like your brother," directed to a small child by the mother, or a teacher telling his third graders, "Lincoln was a great president," are examples of Parent-originated attempts to structure values.

The first level upon which serious questions are asked and serious answers are given, in ethical terms, occurs at what Aiken calls the "moral" level. The difference between claims made at this level and at the first one is that here they can be challenged as factual means-ends claims, or evaluated with regard to moral rules and standards. Aiken points out that valuational discourse at this level often contains elisions and ellipses and thus may appear to be first level expressions.

Valuational statements and ethical decisions can originate in the Parent ego state or in the Adult ego state. As described, the Parent ego state is developed through child imitation of parent or parent surrogate behavior. Therefore, the Parent ego state may contain material (values) that has not been examined for its appropriateness in the present. Rather, it is material that has been learned uncritically from another. When making valuation remarks from the Parent, statements like "This is the way it has always been done" will be heard. Teachers and parents often use such valuation remarks in promoting "valuational sets" in their children and, concurrently, in building the Parent ego in their children. The ethics and values have been learned from others and put into the Parent, but have not been scrutinized by the Adult for the significance now. (Frequently, material from the Parent is referred to as "Parent tapes." The imagery is that of a tape that is put on a tape recorder and run. When a person runs a "Parent tape," he simply plays out the tape.) Thus, when called upon to make an ethical decision or to defend a statement, a person behaving out of Parent "contamination" will use rules and standards from Parent tapes, and may even contrive "facts" based on Parent tapes.

In the introductory example, the teacher may simply say to Tom: "Tom, all students must be treated fairly. I try not to show favoritism in the classroom" or "I always give written exams and it has worked fine in the past and will continue to do so." The key to the Parent value, at this moment, is the unwillingness to examine and test reality. Hence the value remains unscrutinized.

The Adult can also be seen to operate at this level. From this state, which functions to "evaluate stimuli" and enables a person to be more "selective with his response,"[4] evaluations are made on the basis of more objective rules and standards. The Parent tapes might be consulted, but the final decision is made with additional reference to what the community would regard as appropriate according to "moral rules" or to what might be regarded as "factual."

As Perry and Smith assert,[5] problems occur in the classroom when teachers operate at the second level but do not state or clarify the criteria or standards upon which they make valuations and decisions. Valuational statements made without reference to relevant facts or standards may be confusing and frustrating to the student. This fault occurs not only in the teaching of subject material, but also in evaluating and reporting student progress. This gives teaching the appearance of being arbitrary. Though the teacher may have Adult reasons for failing the student, in the absence of an explanation, the student might regard this decision as coming from the Parent of the teacher. This would likely elicit a non-constructive response from the student's Child: "The teacher doesn't like me" or "I'm not smart enough to pass anyway."

Moral and Ethical Level

At the moral level, the soundness of rules and standards used to make decisions and to justify claims is taken for granted. However, at what Aiken calls the "ethical" level, rules and standards become the target of impersonal criticism. Instead of asking the second-level moral question "What ought I to do?," the question at this level would be "What rules and standards ought I to follow?" Such questions may arise out of a conflict of moral values, with changing conditions, or through increased knowledge. In the opening example, the teacher was faced with a conflict between the value of fairness to all and the value of concern for the individual. As in level two, the Adult operates at this level, appealing to Parent data and to the moral standards of the community in choosing an appropriate response. The distinction is that at the ethical level the concern is with principles of values at a higher level. As Perry and Smith suggest,[6] an appeal must be made to principles that define a valuational domain or point of view as a base for criticism of more specific rules and standards. In an educational setting, a principle such as "growth" might guide the instructor in a situation where it is perceived that failing a student might be more of a hindrance than a benefit to the student's academic or economic growth.

When a person asks the question, "Why ought I do what one ought to do?" he has entered the fourth, or "post-ethical," level of moral discourse. At this stage, Aiken points out, a person might say, "I am bound to the rules or morals so long as I am responsive to the demands of a 'rational,' moral being. But nothing can give them authority over my conduct unless I, in virtue of my attitudes and wants, am moved by them."[7]

The key elements of behavior operating at this level are individual responsibility and existential commitment. This is the kind of behavior exhibited by the "autonomous" Adult described by James and Jongeward, or Berne's "integrated" Adult. Berne first refers to integration in this Adult as having ". . . child-like and ethical aspects, but this remains the most obscure area in structural analysis so that it is not possible at present to clarify it clinically. For academic purposes and in order to explain certain clinical phenomena, however, it would be defensible to subdivide the Adult into three areas. Transactionally, this means that anyone functioning as an Adult should ideally exhibit three kinds of tendencies: personal attractiveness and responsiveness, objective data-processing, and ethical responsibility . . . ."[8]

Figure 4.
STRUCTURAL ANALYSIS OF THE ADULT

P

Ethos   Ethical Resonsibility
A2   Data Processing
Pathos   Personal Attractiveness
                              and Responsibility
C

The "Integrated Adult"

The most explicit writing concerning the "integrated Adult" has come from James and Jongeward.[9] (See Figure 4.) The integrated Adult combines the learnings and messages from the Parent with the feelings of the Child ego state. Then a decision is made based on the information from the Parent, Child, and the Adult question of "What is appropriate for the setting? The Adult examination of the Parent value may lead to a reinforcement of that value or a rejection of the Parent value. Harris states: "One function of the freed-up Adult is to examine the Parent so that it may have a choice of accepting or rejecting the Parent data. We must guard against the dogma of rejecting the Parent 'in toto,' and ask, 'Is there anything left worth saving?' "[10] After the examination, the person may continue with the value and "own" it. For example, "I go to church each Sunday now because this is something I feel is important for me and not because I 'have to,' 'should,' or 'must.' " Instead of acting out of a learned program, he has made his own decision. However, after examining his value, the person may reject the value in favor of something that he experiences as more important for him. "Adult ethics" simply means the person is involved in examing his present value system and designing his own ethical code.

The "integrated Adult" involves the person in the process of owning a value system for himself. Instead of an "imitation" or "this is what I'm supposed to think/do," the person is accepting responsibility for his values and the actions resulting from those values.

In their discussion of the "integrated Adult," James and Jongeward discuss the process by which a person integrates the Adult:[11]

(1) Initially, the person is unaware of Parent messages or Child feelings. When faced with an ethical dilemma, he experiences chaos.

(2) Then the person has an Adult awareness of Parent messages and Child feelings.

(3) Next, the person moves to a position of clearly hearing the Parent messages as Parent (and not Adult) and distinguishing Child feelings. (This is referred to as decontamination, or, being able to distinguish between Adult and Parent messages or Child feelings which sound Adult.)

(4) When Adult can distinguish the Parent messages and Child wants, the next step is processing the information and arriving at a plan of action which takes into account the Parent and Child. The Adult is very much in position of a negotiation blending two sets of wants. The desired outcome is a behavior satisfying to both.

(5) Finally, the integration takes place. The result is an action, which takes both the Parent and Child into account.

When the integrated adult operates at the third, or ethical, level of moral discourse, he functions to examine the "Parent of the values of the community" against higher norms. At the post-ethical level, according to Aiken, "man transcends all of his works and is 'free' . . . to junk any and all of them at any time."[12] Using the integrated Adult, man transcends past influences and responds in freedom, redeciding ". . . what is right and what is wrong based on actions that, when examined in their reality, preserve the health and dignity of the person and of the human race."[13]

Classroom Consideration

It should not be taken that the existential posture of the integrated Adult is "best" or is sufficient, but that there is a place in educational settings for the development of existential virtues. By exhibiting the integrated Adult, the teacher provides students with a model of individual commitment to find out what is right or wrong and to examine thoroughly life situations.

As an essential part of education, there are many decisions that must be made by pupils coming from the integrated Adult. As children grow into preadolescence and adolescence, they are confronted with many social questions, such as those concerning war, racial distinction, sex, religion, and ecology. While such problems often evoke serious thinking, they are important also because they can lead into concern for more fundamental principles and speculation. Such a worthy end is not likely with the domineering interruption of the parent's and teacher's Parent. Questions such as these should be met with the integrated Adult, which permits autonomous decision-making. The integrated Adult (in the teacher and in the student) does not offer ready-made decisions or protection from the hazards of making tough decisions; it offers the opportunity for the student to develop habits at being disposed to do whatever he "ought" to do, and to scrutinize "oughts." Without his disposition, a formal knowledge of "oughts" is meaningless.

The integrated Adult response to the ethical dilemma posed in the opening of this chapter would involve, first, listening to Parent messages like, "It is important to be consistent and treat all students alike," and "Each person is unique and different and should be treated as an individual," and, second, being aware of Child feelings, such as confusion or inadequacy as to what to do, and , finally, using this information to raise the Adult question, "Given this situation and these messages, what is the most appropriate response?" The conflict may be seen between the Parent messages (values) and/or between the values expressed in the Parent and the wants and needs of the Child. One integrated Adult response would be for the teacher to discuss the dilemma with the student. By doing this, both teacher and student internalize the problem and scrutinize it. The approach and outcome would be a learning experience for both. The student would gain insight into the difficult position the teacher is in and be active in the decision process. By inviting the student to take part, the teacher takes an existential commitment of trying out something different, though perhaps contrary to the norm of treating everyone equally, and at the same time is aiding in the process of developing the student's integrated Adult. The solution might be to administer an oral exam, but whatever it is, the final outcome will be much more than a grade or a test of knowledge on course material.

Contracting: Moving from Conflict to Problem Solving

Contracting is a process a teacher may use, first, to understand ethical decisions, and then, to solve ethical problems. It may involve the teacher alone, as making a contract with himself, or it may involve the teacher and one or more other participants.

The process for contracting, outlined below, should be seen as a guideline. The sequence of questions may be changed, depending on the demands of a situation. Basically, contracting involves the following steps:

(1) Present Situation. Contracting begins with an awareness that there is some type of conflict. Something is "wrong." In the case of an ethical dilemma, the person is aware of a conflict of values. When teacher or student becomes aware of his involvement in an ethical dilemma, he can ask the following questions: What are my Parent sayings about the dilemma? What are Child feelings about the dilemma?

(2) Desired Situation. This is a question of goals and objectives. Assuming I am in an ethical conflict, what are my goals? What are my desired outcomes? It may be that I hold strongly to my values and do not want to examine them. At that point, the objective may be to learn how to coexist with another set of values or to learn how

to agree to disgree. Or, I may be willing to examine and even compromise one value, in a given situation, for another value.

(3) Problem Solving. This is an action step: How do I get to the desired situation? I have a desired goal; how do I move to that goal? The "integrated Adult" is very involved in designing the plan of action.

(4) Criteria for Success. The criteria for success force the person to raise the question: How will I know if I have been successful? And, in considering the criteria for success, the person may be involved in reconsidering goals, etc.

(5) Recycle. Contracting does not happen in a vacuum. Lots of external events affect the contract, so the recycle step is significant. Recycling simply means doing check outs: Am I getting to my desired goals? If not, how can I redesign step 3? Recycle serves a control function for the contract.

The teacher or student involved with contracting may experience the need to recycle the contract from moment to moment, depending on how the desired goals and the present situation fluctuate. For one time the objectives will be y. This is why the recycle step is significant. It keeps the contracting process up to date. While one type of contract might need to be recycled almost from moment to moment, another contract may be stable and recycled on a weekly, monthly, or yearly basis.

The teacher involved with contracting may not find the process easy. The present situation may be difficult to define, goals and objectives may be unclear, no immediate plan for action may come to mind, or, there may be environmental constraints such as institutional rules and regulations that mediate the contract. However, while not necessarily easy to follow, the steps for contracting provide the teacher with a set of guidelines of how to approach an ethical dilemma.

As an example of how the contracting process might be used, consider the case of Larry F., a high school teacher who devoted one lecture in his biology class to the theory of evolution. Soon afterward, he received some heated phone calls from parents who were disturbed that he was teaching concepts that seemed to be in conflict with their beliefs. The dilemma for Larry was how to teach the theory of evolution without offending or rejecting the individual beliefs of students and their parents. In terms of transactional analysis, Larry was receiving the Parent messages that he should be instructing his students in relevant scientific theories, and that he should respect the beliefs of individuals. These messages lead to Child feelings of confusion and frustration that stemmed from, respectively, the pull between the two messages and tension between the Parent messages and the Child feeling—"leave me alone."

The desired situation would be a solution that satisfied the Parent messages and the Child feelings. Then Larry would not be experiencing frustration and confusion and would instead feel comfortable about having made a "good decision."

The first step to problem solving is to begin to identify options. One option is simply not to discuss the theory of evolution in class, but this avoids the issue of the teacher's wanting to present the theory as important material relevant to the nature of the course. Another option is to present the theory as just that—with the qualification that it is really just a theory and is not necessarily "truth." By presenting the theory as "another point of view," the teacher is giving data to the Adult in his students that they can accept as valid, reject as invalid, or modify in light of whatever prior beliefs there might have been.

In Larry's case, the second option was used. In subsequent lectures on evolution to students, and in talks with parents, he emphasized that he was presenting the theory as an alternative, not as an indoctrination. In this case, the teacher's criterion for success was to stop the frustration and confusion about what he really ought to do. After using the new approach to the topic, and talking with parents and students about it, the teacher reviewed his contract with himself to see how comfortable he was with his dicision. The parents felt more at ease with his new method of presentation, and Larry felt he had made the right decision.

The above example is very qualitative. However, it could involve specific behaviors to be changed with specific criteria for success. How general or how behavioral depends on the teacher's decision with regard to a specific setting.

Contracting is a process that requires individual commitment and responsibility. When problems of value are involved, an individual can use it at the ethical and post-ethical levels in making decisions.

Ethical Decisions: An Exercise

Thus far in this chapter, we have been looking at ways for students and teachers to deal with ethical decisions after they have become aware of the existence of some type of conflict. In this final section, we will consider how the teacher may use transactional analysis to teach students to view ethical decisions in direct ways. In this sense, we are talking about "preventive" behavior, which can provide students with an opportunity to become familiar with skills and tasks that could be helpful in conflict situations. In this manner, the teacher not only is a model but a trainer in "how to approach ethical decisions."

The structured exercise approach to be presented is only one possibility. We invite the teacher to develop creatively other structured approaches that might more appropriately fit their classroom situations.

The objective of the exercise is to get students directly involved in making ethical decisions. As presented here, it involves four steps. The time required for each of the steps may vary from a few minutes to a full class session or more, depending on the teacher and the class, e.g., how significant they feel the topic is and how much time they would like to devote to dealing with it. The steps are: (1) developing a list of ethical issues from the class; (2) ranking those issues to see which are the most significant for the participants; (3) presenting basic transactional analysis theory as a model for understanding ethical decisions; and (4) having the students develop an analysis of a particular ethical decision, perform a role play, and present conflict-resolving options to the rest of the class. Each of these steps will be discussed in detail.

A basic assumption of the first step, the listing of ethical issues, is that if the class develops a list of issues that they see as significant, they will be more involved in the total process. Instead of someone else's saying "Here are the ethical issues for you," they are deciding the ethical issues. This immediately raises the question of what is an "ethical issue"? The teacher may decide at this point to have the class develop a composite of what the word "ethical" means to them, or he may simply provide the definition.

After the concept of "ethical" has been determined, the class can begin to generate ethical issues. We propose a simple procedure of breaking the class down into groups of from four to six participants. These groups have the assignment of brainstorming ethical issues. The basic rule of taking all ideas is important. At the end of ten or fifteen minutes (or whenever the teacher concludes that the brainstorming activity has run "dry"), the various groups come back together and report their lists of issues. The teacher records all the issues developed on a sheet of newsprint. When all the ideas have been recorded, the teacher and class are ready to move on to the next step.

The objective of the second step, ranking the ideas generated in the brainstorming exercise, is to identify those issues that the class feels are the most important at the time. In some settings this step may be skipped if the list of ideas is not long or if all of the issues appear to be equally significant. Here the teacher can play it by ear, perhaps using a simple straw voting process, such as selecting the top five issues. Or, the teacher may want to discuss the significance of various issues raised. While the major purpose of this step is to identify a specific number of issues, there may be a tremendous value in the discussion of which issues should be picked. Whatever approach the teacher decides to use in this step, the objective will be to limit the number of issues to those that seem most important.

The objective of the third step, the introduction of transactional analysis, is to provide the students and teacher with a common model they can use in discussing ethical decisions. The teacher may prepare an introduction to transactional analysis in the form of a short lecture. (Ideally, with time permitting, using some of the written introductions to transactional analysis presented in the discussion so transactional analysis might prove useful.) The teacher might also use an outside resource at this point.[14]

The teacher might prepare some simple examples about Parent, Adult, Child, and briefly discuss the definition of each. A question and answer session may also be held with the students, but again, the key element is time. If there is sufficient time, an entire session might be devoted to discussing transactional analysis. If not, a brief five-minute lecture might be adequate.

The fourth step is having the students put together the transactional model and the ethical issues they have identified. Again, the teacher has several options. The simplest might be to break the group into groups of from four to six students. Each group would have one ethical issue to investigate, and would have to identify the value conflicts that characterize the issue. They would be asked to listen for Parent messages as well as Child feelings as the values are identified, and to write them down. Once the conflicts have been analyzed, each group would develop a role play that illustrates the ethical dilemma. They would then present this role play to the class and offer suggestions for options that might be used, i.e., integrated Adult responses. Following each presentation, the role play and ethical issue would be discussed and the rest of the class would be invited to offer options.

When the teacher feels that the class has had time to perform the investigation and prepare the role play, the groups should be called back together with each group given an opportunity to present its role play and options. The teacher would occupy the important position of referee to the discussion, while also keeping the discussion flowing and eliciting the various options.

An option that can be tagged on to the end of this exercise is to have the students take the choices presented to them in various sessions and recycle their role plays.

The overlying objective of the exercise is to involve students directly in the process of identifying and analyzing ethical dilemmas, and developing some ways to respond to them. As the students become involved in the various steps, they are performing behavioral rehearsals, and practicing how they might deal with ethical decisions outside of the classroom setting.

We again encourage the teacher to view the exercise as an opportunity to create various new renditions.

Summary

In this chapter, we have presented transactional analysis as a useful framework for students and teachers to understand ethical dilemmas. In examining it, the levels of moral discourse were discussed. Our reasons for viewing transactional analysis and the levels of moral discourse were to show: (1) the relationship between moral levels and Parent, Adult, and Child; (2) that an appeal to any one level of moral discourse should be directed to certain ego states; and (3) that persons behaving out of the integrated Adult are capable of higher levels of moral decision-making.

In addition to understanding ethical dilemmas, we have suggested two tools. The first, contracting, is a way of moving from ethical dilemmas to problem solving. It provides a process by which the teacher and student may examine the dilemma and make decisions for action. The second tool is a suggested structured exercise for the teacher interested in engaging students in identifying ethical issues and developing options for responses to ethical issues. The exercise provides the students with an opportunity to practice or rehearse various responses to ethical issues. In addition, it provides the student with an opportunity to learn new behaviors without the negative consequences that may come in situations outside of the classroom.

We believe that a teacher operating out of the "integrated Adult" is a powerful model for his students. In doing so, the teacher shows a way in which students can deal with ethical conflicts. It is hoped that these concepts will be helpful to the teacher as well as the student in understanding his own ethical code and its application in an educational setting.

[1]The reader interested in pursuing transactional analysis literature is referred to the following: Berne, Eric, *Transactional Analysis in Psychotherapy*. New York: Castle Books, 1961; Berne, Eric, *Games People Play*. New York: Castle Books, 1964; *Berne, Eric, Principles of Group Treatment*. New York: Grove Press, 1966; *Berne, Eric, What Do You Say After You Say Hello?* New York: Grove Press, 1972; Harris, Thomas, *I'm OK—You're OK. New York:* Harper & Row, 1967; Holloway, W. and Holloway, M. *Change Now*. Akron, Ohio: Midwest Institute for Human Understanding, 1973; James, M. and Jongeward, D., *Born To Win*. Reading, Mass.: Addison-Wesley, 1971; Steiner, Claude , *Scripts People Live*. New York: Grove Press, 1974.

[2]Holloway and Holloway, *op. cit.*, p. 6.

[3]H. D. Aiken. *Reason and Conduct* (New York: Alfred A. Knopf, 1962).

[4]James and Jongeward, *op. cit.*, p. 128.

[5]James F. Perry and Phillip G. Smith, "Levels of Valuational Discourse in Education," in *Theories of Values and Problems of Education*, ed. Phillip G. Smith (Urbana, Ill.:   University of Illinois Press, 1970), p. 118.

[6]Ibid., p. 120.

[7]Aiken, *op. cit.*, p. 85.

[8]Berne, *Transactional Analysis in Psychotherapy*, p. 194—95.

[9]James and Jongeward, *op. cit.*, pp. 258—63.

[10]Harris, *op. cit.*, pp. 217—22.

[11]James and Jongeward, *op. cit.*, p. 259.

[12]Aiken, *op. cit.*, p. 85.

[13]James and Jongeward, *op. cit.*, p. 272.

[14]The International Transactional Association (1772 Vallejo Street, San Francisco, California 94123)   has a geographic listing of persons who have been trained in transactional analysis.

10

The Morality of Counseling: Implications for Teachers

Susan Stanford
Peter Gillan

Counseling, like teaching, is carried on by a variety of practitioners, both amateurs and professionals. At one time or another, almost everyone becomes a counselor to another person. Parents may assume such a role with their children, or with each other. People try to help friends solve personal problems. Neighbors counsel each other. Young people practice on their peers. Employers often intervene in the personal lives of their workers. Professionals, such as ministers, physicians, lawyers, bankers, journalists, undertakers, social workers and, especially, teachers, find their relationships with clients opportunities to assume counseling responsibilities. With the growth of professional counseling and the publicity given to popular theories and techniques, counseling by amateurs is affecting the lives of more and more people, frequently with serious adverse results.

The impact of counseling, by professionals as well as by amateurs, can have moral consequences—for both practitioners and clients. Because it aims to help individuals to make choices relative to goals and alternative courses of personal action, it deals with the vital ingredients of which morality is made—human needs, personal desires, cultural traditions, and the interplay of conscience among these often conflicting compulsions. The consequences of the counselor's influence may be negative and traumatic. Consequently, all who are tempted to assume such roles confront critical considerations about the morality of counseling.

Concept of Professional Morality

Educational professionals influence human behavior through four key direct processes: teaching, counseling, remediation therapy, and administration. Indirect influences come through such functions as theory construction, research, curriculum designing, and of course, evaluation. All such interventions into the lives of students have moral implications. Of these, the most controversial concern, perhaps, has been with the moral impact of counseling.

Morality in professional practice is a product of dual mandates. On the one hand, the general moral guidelines functioning in the culture operate as measures of behavior; on the other, codes of professional ethics provide guidelines to follow. The professional is expected to be a "moral person"—not just because it is a condition of social membership, but, additionally, because professionals are viewed as model figures, an expection that applies particularly to teachers and counselors. One mark of a profession is the rules for practice that govern specifically professional behavior. The latter, or what might be called *professional morality*, relates to the services provided to and relationships maintained with clients.

The professional morality of counseling has high visibility because of the nature of the services provided. The counselor influences the social, emotional, and psychological adjustments of clients, bringing about changes in behavior that are readily discernable. Such intervention into the lives of others is a serious responsibility, equal in effect at times to the impact of medical surgery.

Morality of Intervention

Apart from the results achieved, or the professional techniques employed, is the prior question concerning whether intervention, itself, is a moral process. The query stems from concern about individual freedom and the integrity of selfhood. It raises for examination, too, the goals of counseling, including its moral commitments to the society as a whole and the client served.

Whether or not counseling as a process violates the integrity of selfhood is a fundamental consideration. The concept of self-determinism is deeply rooted in the tenets of any free society. En parentis authority, of course, gives parents and teachers the right to direct, control, or otherwise influence the behavior of children and youth. Out of such practice comes the key question: Is it moral for counselors to assume such responsibilities? If not, the consideration becomes one of client consent. In the field of medicine, it is unethical to perform an operation or modify the physical health of a patient without authorization from the client or a legal guardian. Does the same ethic hold for professional services that may change a person's social, emotional, or mental health? In school situations, particularly, many students are required to undergo counseling, with or without their consent. With non-professional counselors, permission to intervene often is more tacit than explicit. Even with professional counselors in non-school situations, the client may not give written consent for treatment, except in those cases where the individual becomes an institutionalized patient. Such loose accountability opens questions about the morality of intervention that all who practice counseling need to consider.

The goals of counseling relate to the right of intervention, as do the motives of those who practice. Is the function of counseling, for example, to modify individual behavior to conform to goals held by the counselor or the educational institution, or to particular cultural traditions? Does counseling aim to promote independence in clients? Is the counselor more concerned with satisfying personal needs or those of counselees? Answers to these and other questions are pertinent to judgments about the morality of intervention.

Controversy has long prevailed regarding whether counseling intervention into the behavior of an individual is morally permissible. Professional counselors, of course, agree that it is, but they differ with respect to the amount and kinds of influences that should be exercised, even with client consent. Albert Ellis's theory of Rational Emotive Therapy assumes the prerogative to influence behavior through direct and positive means. At the opposite end of the continuum would be Carl Rogers, with his non-directive or client-centered theory that endeavors to place responsibility for behavioral change on the individual being counseled. The latter seems to be more sensitive to whether intervention, and how much, can be morally justified.

Claude Steiner takes the position that it is actually unethical not to intervene once a client-counselor relationship has been established. He feels that:

> The myth of the desirability of non-directive, non-manipulative therapy persists among both laymen and professionals, and needs to be dispelled. It has long been suspected, and it is now generally accepted, that no therapist can hope to avoid imposing her system of values upon the people she works for. The issue of manipulation has now become simply a question of whether a therapist, consciously and overtly is willing to expose people to his values or whether he prefers to do it without his own and his client's awareness. . . . [1]

Professional Morality: Guidelines for Teachers Who Counsel

Professional morality defines the rules for the practice of counseling, as contrasted to social morality that prescribes mandates for living. Those teachers who find themselves counselors to students should be aware of some of the moral guidelines of counseling. Conformity, as with all moral conduct, is the major criterion for judgment. The morality of counseling, however, is less clearly defined than the rules for professional behavior in some other fields, such as law or medicine. In the absence of specific prescriptions, teachers who counsel may find themselves operating in areas where moral guidelines are non-existent or conflicting.

Illustrations of the kind of moral guidelines that teachers should follow include the following:

(1)   Teachers who counsel are committed to promote healthy adjustment for the student in the pursuit of personal goals within the context of established moral traditions. Each counselor wishes to help the student solve the problems confronting him. The counselor acts as a catalyst in aiding the student to see the various alternative courses of action open to him, the consequences of each and then to make an appropriate choice based on this assessment. But the teacher who counsels is morally bound to advise the student in line with the established mores and principles of society.   One major criticism leveled at many counselors today is that too often the student has been encouraged to "do his own thing" without any regard to the established values of the society. The moral counselor then must be supportive of the personal change that the student wishes to bring about, but he must do so in full recognition of the accepted societal norms.

(2)   Teachers who counsel should restrict professional services to areas and levels of personal training and competence. Counseling is an art and a skill. Professionals in the practice of this skill need to receive adequate and appropriate training. The case of the college professor who spent two weeks at a Gestalt workshop on the west coast, and then returned to run groups in his home, advertising himself as an expert in Gestalt experiences, constitutes a moral violation.   Two weeks of training in anything hardly qualifies one as an expert. The professor above may have been well-intentioned, but he was not a professional counselor and he could have faced some serious trouble if the participants in his group decided to "open up." Each counselor must protect himself from areas where he is not sufficiently trained. He should deal with those areas that he feels are closest to his areas of

competence. When a student brings in a problem that a teacher does not feel competent to handle, he must be referred to someone who can.

(3) Teachers who counsel should use counseling techniques of *proven* professional effectiveness. The moral counselor should follow a professional procedure that is endorsed by the field. Just as it is immoral for a surgeon to deviate from the accepted ways and standards of removing a vital organ, so, too, should the counselor respect and practice those techniques of counseling that have been researched and tested to show proven success. If a surgeon decided to treat chest pain by removing a gall bladder, he would soon be liable for a malpractice suit. Similarly, the teacher who tries to aid a student who is having problems relating with her parents by inexplicably hypnotizing the student is acting immorally. All practicing professionals, whether they are dealing with the physical or the psychological health of an individual under their care, must adhere to the recognized techniques of treatment within their profession.

Some Sins of Counseling: Considerations for Teachers

Counseling as a moral force in the lives of students comes under fire because practitioners "play God" with the lives of their students, telling them what to do and prescribing specific moral standards for them. At the other extreme, counselors are accused of assuming the role of the "devil's observer" of the problems people have, allowing them to flounder in confusion, frustration, and frequently, destructive guilt feelings, while providing no moral guidelines to help. In between these two contrasting indictments are a variety of charges, all of which raise serious questions about the moral mission of counseling, whether it be practiced by professional counselors or by teachers in classrooms.

All who counsel should be aware of the more common "sins" that have been identified. Such criticisms are to be expected, perhaps since counseling is a relatively new field, standards of qualification are low and in some states non-existent, and research to verify procedures and results is meager. No approach to counseling has been exempt from one or more of these indictments. More than other professional services in the field of education, e. g., teaching, remedial therapy, and administration, counseling has been accused of actually contributing to the loss of morality. This charge is not widely applicable, but the fact remains that some counselors have, by direction and nondirection, advocated abandonment of traditional moral standards in favor of guidelines improvised by individuals to fit each occasion. People wonder, too, whether counseling helps students to develop their abilities or simply to rationalize their failure to do so.

New experiments in group counseling seem to be producing as many maladjustments as they are curing. The fad, as it is now called in many quarters, is being oversold by advocates who seem more interested in the financial rewards and publicity than the results achieved. People who join such groups for renewal or self-discovery too frequently learn to their regret that once they have taken themselves apart, like Humpty Dumpty, they cannot put themselves back together again. All of this is damaging to the field of professional counseling, particularly because some of its leaders have become advocates of such group therapy sessions.

As mentioned, perhaps one of the cardinal sins of counseling, all other criticisms notwithstanding, is to fail to provide help when it is needed. The counselor may abdicate such responsibilities—sometimes through referral, sometimes by refusing to listen or to provide time. The failure may be due to excessive non-direction on the part of the counselor or to the imposition of arbitrary solutions that do not fit the student's needs. Whatever the reason, professional counselors as professionals in the field of medicine have a responsibility to be of service when called upon for help.

Another of the cardinal sins of counseling would certainly be reflected by the teacher who chooses to counsel an individual in an area that is not his expertise. This sin is particularly relevant to consider, for when the teacher is approached by a student for help, a first consideration is whether the problem is within the range of professional qualifications. For example, when a student seems very depressed, or shows signs of taking drugs, the teacher has a moral obligation to refer the student to someone appropriately trained to deal with these problems.

Another sin of counseling occurs when the counselor starts to impose a personal value system on the student. The student has come to the counselor to work out a problem that he has not been able to solve on his own. It is not the counselor's job to tell him how to solve his problem without considering the whole student, including values held and the total life pattern. To do so would be solving the problem by the counselor's own standards, discounting the importance or existence of the student's views or subcultural life style. Rather, as a counselor the teacher must act as a catalyst, helping the student to discover and explore the various alternatives open and the consequences of each.

It has often been said that some people are drawn to working in the field of counseling because they are trying to solve their own personal problems. Another variation of the same motivation occurs when the teacher is guilty of exploiting the student's problem to meet personal needs or ambitions. It is recognized that each professional person needs some gratification from his work, but this must never be attained at the expense of the student. For example, the counselor who encourages discipleship among students, rather than self-determination, is acting immorally. The counselor who fosters the feeling that students cannot function without help, or that the advisor has the answers to all counselees' problems is clearly guilty of misuse of clients. Not all teachers are guilty of ignoring ethical and moral standards when they sit down to talk with a student; it is always the minority of practitioners who undermine public confidence in the majority. It is also true that no one counseling strategy holds all the answers, nor will any good counselor use one strategy exclusively with all students. To do so would be unprofessional inasmuch as the needs of counselees differ, and one individual may need one kind of help at one time and another kind with a different type of problem.

Should Teachers Counsel?

The question of whether a teacher should function as a counselor seems to be never fully answered. Twenty years ago, Donald Arbuckle, writing of a concept he called the "teacher-counselor," strongly advocated the position.[2] He argued that as the teacher has greatest access to the students, he should function as the counselor. Recently, however, Arbuckle has almost totally reversed his position, expounding that all counseling should be left to properly trained counselors. He states: "The teacher is not a counselor or a psychotherapist, either from the point of view of education or knowledge, and it is doubtful that his functions (should) include becoming involved in a real counseling relationship with a child."[3]

In theory, there are things that a teacher should or should not do. Ideally, one can argue that a teacher should teach the students, and the school counselor should work with the students' problems, but, realistically, nothing in life is ever that cut and dried. Many teachers have at some point—in the locker room, on the play field, or at the lunch break—had a student approach them with a personal problem. In such a case the teacher could say he does not want to talk, tell the student to see the school counselor (if there is one), or offer to listen to the student. Very often the type of teacher to whom a student will be drawn is one who shows a sincere interest in students. Caring about them, while providing an atmosphere of optimum learning, may encourage students to seek help in solving personal problems.

No student is problem-free and the types of problems faced include a lack of motivation for a class requirement, test anxiety, discipline problems, or more personal, emotional problems. Students are growing individuals trying to cope with more than just academic learning, and problems are part of such growth. The sensitive teacher realizes the impact that problems can have on a student's life and is aware of how difficult it is for one to function scholastically if problems exist, but there are several important issues that should be considered regarding whether teachers should counsel.

Approachability-Availability and Role Differentiation

The teacher, by the mere fact of seeing students in class every day, is often far more approachable in the student's mind than a school counselor. By asking the student a simple question, such as why his homework was not completed, the teacher may casually, but unintentionally, unearth a problem in the home. The student may be too scared to go to a counselor to talk about the problem, but the teacher's initiating question, as one of caring as well as concern, gives him the opportunity to discuss his problem. In some schools, counselors do not even exist. Either for financial reasons or because of the particular philosophy of the principal or school district, the school may not have a full time counselor. In these unfortunate situations, teachers do not even have a backup resource to which they can refer student problems.

The issue of a teacher's time is another important aspect to be considered. Most teachers have very busy schedules, with classes to prepare, papers to correct, meetings, and conferences with parents. To expect a teacher to add to a full time load by taking on a string of counselees could surely be seen as unethical. It is not only unfair to the teacher but also unfair for the student to hope that he could have much private time with the teacher.

Ideally, the teacher and the counselor have similar concerns for their students. Both should have an interest in their students' learning and growth and an empathy and willingness to listen to their students. Additionally, it is hoped that neither the teacher nor the counselor are judgmental of their students or force them to take their advice. Such behavior could lead to resentment for or greater dependence on the teacher or counselor.

The fact that such commonalities exist does not, however, negate the role differences that should be recognized. The teacher is a person who imparts knowledge, i.e., subject matter, to the student, serving as a facilitator and inviting the student to learn certain data. The counselor, of course, attempts to guide the student in the educational process, often dealing with the personal functioning of the individual. Briefly explained, the student relates with his world and the significant aspects of it. The counselor helps the student to adjust both to himself and to his world in order to make functioning in it more comfortable. He listens to the student, accepts personal problems without value-judging, and helps to facilitate the resolution of the problems within the student's value system and the necessary confines of society.

A number of years ago, Arbuckle elaborated on the area of role confusion.[4] He said: "There are those who will say that the teacher cannot be an effective counselor because of his disciplinarian role. Others may say that the teacher has a friendly relationship with the students, whereas one must maintain a professional relationship in order to do effective counseling." All counselors should be both professional and non-judgmental. If this objectivity is compromised by a teacher doing counseling, then it would be wiser for the teacher to refer the student. Ira Gordon points out that although teaching and counseling are not exactly the same, ". . . the goals are essentially the same although the emphasis may differ and the degree of deep-feeling involvement may be quite different." He concludes by saying: "There can be no such dichotomy as having teaching concerned only with intellectual processes and counseling with emotional processes. Both are concerned with the whole person in dynamic interaction with his world."[5]

Confidentiality and Ethics

The confidentiality issue is of prime importance in the overall student-teacher relationship. A major premise in any service professional is the understanding by the client that what they choose to share with their professional advisor (doctor, lawyer, clergyman, counselor, etc.) will remain totally confidential. This same right must be recognized by every teacher who learns any private information from or about a student. Too often we have heard of cases where information confidentially shared with one teacher very quickly travels the grapevine and becomes common knowledge. The teacher must treat students' confidences with a sacredness that is implicit in the function of a counselor. Each student is a full-fledged human being in his own right. Teachers and counselors alike need to respect fully the rights of each student. This most essentially includes their right to privacy and the expectation that their confidences will be kept. Gordon presents five areas that both teachers and counselors must respect without exception:[6]

(1) Each teacher-counselor has a moral obligation to safeguard the confidence, individuality, and integrity of the child.

(2) Each teacher-counselor has a responsibility to use information in such a way that it will not be harmful to the child.

(3) Each teacher-counselor must be careful not to exceed the limits of his professional training and competence in his efforts to be of service to the child.

(4) Each teacher-counselor must be careful not to exercise the power latent in his position to judge, impose his own values upon, make decisions for, and manipulate the child.

(5) Each teacher-counselor must be careful to safeguard written information, and to provide such information to

other agencies only with the consent of the child or after satisfactory assurance has been given of the use to be made of this information.

One of the reasons a student may turn to a counselor for help is the objectivity that he offers. At times one needs to talk about problems with an impartial person. It helps to give perspective to a situation. However, a teacher cannot be classified as totally uninvolved, having already known the individual as a student. In instructional relationships, perceptions and feelings about students naturally develop. If some of these feelings are negative, the teacher may have difficulty transmitting the important ingredient of "acceptance" when counseling a student. We are not suggesting that all counselors love their clients. We are asking simply whether some teachers may be too emotionally involved to offer the best help to their students.

Does Counseling Conflict with Evaluation?

Another question to consider is whether a teacher's evaluation of a student may be affected by private information learned. Ideally, teachers are sensitive to which of their students may be grappling with personal problems, but as one of the teacher's functions is to evaluate the student, the grade given might be affected by personal knowledge about this student. Would a teacher tend to be more lenient in grading if he knows a student's father is an alcoholic, or more severe if he learns that a student has just stolen a watch? What are the ethical implications if evaluation is so influenced? Information obtained outside the classroom can change the teacher-student relationship. In gaining private information, the teacher needs to be wary of leniency, favoritism, or manipulation occuring as a consequence.

A teacher is expected to represent the norms of society. The school that hires the teacher and the parents who support that school want the teacher to help socialize the child. But what happens when the needs of the child are in conflict with the needs of the school? To whom is a teacher first educationally accountable?

It is recognized that the school is the employer of the teacher as well as the counselor. By accepting employment, both the teacher and counselor agree to uphold the goals of the school. However, as previously discussed, one of the major premises of the service professions rests on the issue of confidentiality's being honored. If either a teacher or a counselor does not respect this issue and treats the breaking of confidentiality lightly, the very function for which the counselor was hired and in which the teacher frequently participates will never be achieved. No student will ever go to a teacher/counselor if he feels anything said will be repeated to the administrators, other teachers, or peers. Similar to the "privileged communications" rights of physicians and lawyers, we would offer that the rights of the students be taken into account first and foremost in this area. Confidentiality should be broken only when there is a serious risk to a third party. It is important to mention that, wherever possible, the rights of the school and the student should be respected together and everything possible done to protect them.

It is almost impossible today for any teacher to steer completely away from doing counseling. If one views counseling as a process of helping individuals to learn how to make decisions regarding problems or alternatives they face, then teachers will find themselves much involved. However, just which roles the counselor and the teacher play in a student's development is sometimes difficult to compartmentalize, for ultimately the aim of education is to help the student to negotiate better with his world. It is a teaching process, one that reeducates and produces change. It is a dynamic process, where one person (the teacher or counselor) tries to help another person (the student) increase personal capacity to function successfully in the world. In theory, the teacher and the counselor have separate functions as facilitators in the student's growth, but because it is not always easy to keep these differentiated, an important question is whether a teacher should receive specialized training in counseling skills.

Developing Counseling Skills

The ability to counsel is not something with which an individual is born; nor is it something that magically becomes part of an individual as teaching maturity is attained. Counseling is both an art and a science. The professional skill must be learned if it is to be done well—and it must be practiced. It would be impractical for teachers to take a full program of counseling courses when what they really want to do is to teach.

Earlier, we said that the classroom experience for the student is, it is to be hoped, an open, warm, encouraging, and non-threatening one. Therefore, a major argument could be made that the basis of a student-teacher relationship should be a dynamic interpersonal relationship. Many of the skills that a counselor receives in professional training, e.g., active listening, empathy, perception of feelings, and non-punitive support, are desirable components of any interpersonal relationship. Training in human relations skills could aid the teacher to develop a better classroom environment. In such an environment, students would be encouraged to refine their feelings of self-worth by knowing that their thoughts and needs are important.

Another advantage of teachers' taking professional preparation in counseling is the enhancement that can come in interschool personnel relationships. Ideally, the best way for any school to function is to have all of its professional employees and staff view themselves working together as a team. Any team works best when each member knows his own responsibility and what each colleague is doing. Therefore, with their two jobs so closely intertwined, the teacher and the counselor would do well to know accurately what the other is doing. Such mutual knowledge could help to foster communication and to dispel misperceptions.

It is important to remember that a teacher is not a full-fledged counselor. For this reason, no teacher should be expected to handle all levels of counseling problems that may be confronted. All teachers should know to whom they may refer students who have come to them with serious problems. This again points up the need for good intercommunication among school personnel. Teachers need to be aware of their resources and back-up support.

Lack of extensive training time and many of the other variables cited above require that a teacher be aware of when to make a referral and the best method for doing so.

Twenty years ago, Ruth Strang, who was then at Columbia Teachers College, pointed out five situations in which a teacher should negotiate referral.[7] These are still true today:

(1) Health and physical conditions that require the attention of a nurse or doctor.
(2) Severe emotional disturbance, indicated by extreme preoccupation and persistent daydreaming or flight from reality, unhappiness or depression, thoughts of suicide, extreme overconscientiousness, withdrawal from social contacts, lack of interest in anything, feeling of guilt or personal responsibility for everything that goes wrong, extreme neglect of personal appearance, very marked distractability, unfounded suspicion and fear.
(3) Deep-rooted problems in home conditions.
(4) A prolonged deviation from the usual pattern of behavior—for instance, from sociability to unfriendliness.
(5) Problems too deep for expression—inability to talk over the difficulty—to put it into words.

No teacher should consider a referral as a personal failure to handle a problem. Rather, each referral should be viewed as an action to bring about the optimum growth for the student. If the "team" members themselves are all working to achieve this goal, then, surely, referral will be made in the best possible manner with the least possible side effects.

Implications for the Teacher-Counselor

The decision by a teacher to assume the role of counselor is a crucial one. A first priority should be the determination of when to counsel and when to refer a problem to a professional colleague who is better qualified to handle it. Certain kinds of counseling are natural for teachers; other problems usually are outside the range of professional competence and responsibility of persons without professional preparation in counseling.

Moral and Mechanical Counseling

Whether or not to counsel may depend on the nature of the problem presented by a student. If moral decisions are involved, the teacher must evaluate personal qualifications for providing help. Many of the counseling problems that come to classroom teachers, however, are more mechanical than moral. An example of a non-moral counseling service would be providing advice to a student about the choice of courses to study, the development of study skills, or the perfection of behavioral habits. Such problems are academic and learning-oriented in nature—natural responsibilities of teachers. Almost all teachers can help with them.

Educational counseling does not require highly developed counseling skills, although such skills may make the service more effective, nor is it of a substantive moral nature. Knowledge of a student's value system or moral standards is unnecessary in order to help him solve a complicated chemistry problem. This type of value-free problem may exist also in a student's social life. For a student who has trouble making friends or being accepted by peers, the teacher/counselor might be able to give advice about interpersonal communication or suggest ways to be assertive. For the most part, the information or suggestions given to the student are based on facts (". . . the word is dog . . .") or scientific data about behavior (". . . active listening is an important part of two-way communication . . . ").

Providing information does not require the teacher to be a counselor; nor is the influence necessarily moral in nature. The teacher is simply helping the student to read, to communicate better with people, or perhaps to increase problem-solving abilities. Yet the fact that such help is seen as desired is, in itself, a value judgment. Anything that defines what a person should or should not do may have moral implications. In fact, anything one does in society is influenced by established moral guidelines. Because of the general and almost universal acceptance of some values, it does not seem necessary to argue about the morality of trying to help a student learn to read or communicate.

Teachers frequently are confronted with other types of problems, however, that have moral implications. A critical need of the teacher/counselor is to be able to differentiate between value-oriented and mechanical problems. What does a teacher do whose values differ from those of a student who seeks help with a problem that has moral overtones? Should a teacher attempt to counsel in an area that is charged with controversy, such as drug use, sexual behavior, birth control, or partisan politics? For example, how should a teacher handle the student who confides that he was the one who cost the school $600 by setting off the fire alarm three days in a row? The problem may be so complicated that it requires more than discipline. Such students may be crying out for attention. What about the student who cheats on an exam or the one who fails to footnote a major part of a written report? Then there are the touchier problems that brush the realm of religious beliefs. How much of a right or responsibility does a teacher/counselor have to intervene in a student's life? Should the pregnant high school senior be approached and given counsel?

Guidelines for the Teacher-Counselor

Students are continually facing moral conflicts—it is part of being human. The observant teacher will see these conflicts happening and at times will be asked to help resolve them. Each teacher/counselor has a personal set of values, but to force these on someone else is to act as a moralist and not as a counselor. The key word here is force. A teacher/counselor does not have to hide individual moral commitments. If asked, they may be shared but it is important to remember than the student usually turns to counseling for help in resolving his *own* values conflicts. The teacher/counselor should function as a catalyst and a facilitator in this process. A counselor, even a professional one, should not function as a religious leader or moralist. If that is what the student is looking for, he should be referred to a person with the needed expertise. As mentioned before, one of the guidelines of counseling is for a counselor to work within professional competencies.

What are some of the types of counseling a teacher can undertake with reasonable confidence that the student can be helped rather than hurt? One safe area, as cited, and one in which teachers have considerable competence, is educational and/or learning problems. If a student has difficulty reading or grasping abstract mathematical or chemical concepts, the need may be for reinforcement of study skills or improvement of a poor self-image. Teachers can supply this without undue risk. By assisting the student to become more proficient in his studies, a teacher may actually build self-confidence for dealing with problems outside of school—a key goal of counseling.

In some classrooms, students have to cooperate with each other to carry on learning activities; thus, assistance in learning how to work with others might be another area of counseling open to the teacher. It is no secret that a major portion of this country's socialization process goes on within school walls. Some children's first contacts with other children their age occur when they start school, where children are confronted with having to work in groups and needing to adjust to peer pressures as well as other social demands. Some students find these adaptations easier than do others. Students who have problems in the classroom are the ones most likely to have problems outside of school. A teacher who can help such a student to adjust will be affecting his overall ability to relate to other people—and this is what counseling endeavors to do.

Helping a student to develop the skills needed to chart his educational career and planning the training related to personal goals are tasks closely related to teaching. One of the most important skills that a student can develop in school is the ability to learn when no one is directing him. A teacher can help a student to discover his talents and strengths and to analyze areas of need as well as competence. A student can be aided to explore where he wants to go with his education or his life and to look at the alternate ways to get there. A teacher can help the student to look at the realistic constraints and limitations that the world imposes as well as the different options the students might have for overcoming them. Helping a student to learn this type of basic problem-solving approach could prove invaluable when he is confronted with new situations and problems of maturation. The way a teacher helps the students to learn to solve problems is not by spending time offering individualized therapy sessions, but through the approach employed in classroom learning. Do the students rely on the teacher for the answers or are they encouraged to learn how to learn and then apply such skills to problems outside of the classroom? This is a key question related to the development of personal independence—another goal of counseling.

What are some of the areas that might fall outside of a teacher's counseling ability? When students come to teachers with problems of personal adjustment, sexual experiences, drug use, gang life, family relationships, religion, and what might be called "life style," are teachers the proper counselors? Teachers are not trained to handle this type of involvement with students. One of the biggest sins of counseling is to lead someone into the unknown. If the teacher does not know where the counseling is leading the student or if confidence in professional skills is lacking, the efforts may hurt rather than help. It is part of a teacher's professional responsibility to recognize areas of personal expertise and limits of individual competence. When a teacher begins to dabble beyond such limits, not only may the counseling be a failure, but teaching effectiveness may be diminished as well. The challenge to each teacher is to know personal limitations and to keep within them.

Summary

Counseling is a basic and important professional service—one with moral implications for both practitioners and clients. All who assume such roles need to consider seriously the moral consequences of their efforts, however well-intentioned they may be. A counselor, along with other professionals, confronts two sets of moral guidelines: one imposed by the culture to assure its survival, and another maintained by the professional group for the same reason, namely, to protect clients and the integrity of the service provided by members. Accepting the role of counselor carries the obligation to abide by this dual moral mandate.

Whether teachers should counsel may be a moot question. They do; some with effectiveness and others in ways harmful to students. Teaching and counseling are so closely intertwined that in a real sense to teach well is to counsel, and vice versa. But counseling carries special professional responsibilities that teachers who undertake it should assume. Those who find themselves selected by students as counselors and who feel inclined to respond have the obligation to develop the skills and knowledge essential to effective practice.

Certain kinds of counseling, more than others, are more safely carried out by classroom teachers. These are related closely to the teaching function in which professional competence prevails. Client problems in areas such as drug use, sexual behavior, and religion should referred to professional counselors who are better prepared to deal with such matters. The challenge to the classroom teacher is to keep counseling services within personal areas of expertise.

[1]Claude M. Steiner, *Scripts People Live* (New York: Grove Press, 1974), pp. 275—76.

[2]Donald S. Arbuckle, *Guidance and Counseling in the Classroom* (Boston: Allyn & Bacon, 1957), p. 14.

[3]Donald S. Arbuckle, *Counseling: Philosophy, Theory, and Practice* (Boston: Allyn & Bacon, 1965), pp. 187—88.

[4]Donald S. Arbuckle, *Teacher Counseling* (Cambridge, Mass.: Addison-Wesley Press, 1950).

[5]Ira Gordon, *The Teacher as a Guidance Worker* (New York: Harper Bros., 1956) p. 269.

[6]Ibid., p. 293.

[7]Ruth Strang, *The Role of the Teacher in Personnel Work*, 4th ed. (New York: Bureau of Publications, Teachers College, Columbia University, 1953).

11

To Train or to Educate: A Moral Decision

B. Claude Mathis

The ethos of any society can be judged by *what* and *how* its teachers teach. When the emphasis is on the mastery of specific behaviors and the performance of prescribed tasks, the social concern is weighted more toward material and technological progress. If the focus is more on meaning, on *why* concepts are important, on the use made of skills and knowledge, and upon the priorities human behavior should serve, the social character may be said to be humanistically oriented. Whatever the direction of social influences and the responses made by teachers to them, the decisions are moral ones.

Implicit in the way any society asks its teachers to nurture the development of its young are basic moral values considered essential to perpetuate its way of life and moral system. Thus, the need to transmit the culture is at the root of all formal systems of education and teaching. Cultures, however, can have many faces. Because educational institutions attempt to mirror the totality of our culture, dissonance and conflicts inevitably emerge.

An Amoral Tradition

A priority of our educational system in the United States has been to resolve problems of cultural diversity and disparate moral values. The approach has been practical, the efforts often skillful, but the results have been frustratingly unsuccessful. What has emerged is an omnibus approach to education and teaching that endeavors to provide "something for everyone" without being too much concerned with the moral consequences of promises made. For example, from the contrasting benchmarks of local control of public school systems, commitments to the supposed diversity that options in parochial and private schools offer, and the wide ranges of post-secondary types of institutions and services, education in the United States endeavors to operate in a moral vaccuum. Schools and teachers shy away from the big issues that undergird the philosophies, methods, and learning theories they follow. In doing so, they avoid confronting such crucial questions as: what is right or wrong in our society; or what is good or bad in human conduct. Such superficiality gives education a posture of calculated amorality, supported principally by the tradition of the constitutional doctrine of separation of church and state. The moral evasion is encouraged further by the growing dominance of the scientific ethic that social values evolve within various societal groups.

An examination of the formal systems of education in the United States over the past century would produce similar conclusions by astute observers regarding the philosophy and values that have shaped the directions taken by teachers and educators in our attempts to provide education for all. Even as we now move, in Cross's terms, toward supplying an education for each,[1] we can observe more of a replication of the traditional habits than the initiation of solutions that seek a new ethic of commitment in learning.

The key conclusions reached in common by careful observers of past traditions in American education and teaching can be summarized as follows:

(1)   The various systems of education in the United States, both public and private and at all levels, represent a macrocosm of concentration on those learnings that address the questions of *how* the learner performs specific behaviors

and *when* the performance is appropriate, given particular conditions. Such concentration on learning how and when to perform or behave is a dominant theme in teaching. The question of why one should learn how and when to do something is neglected or given only minor importance. Consequently, the classroom is much more an arena for learning how to manipulate the culture in the interest of maximizing a position of status in one's reference group than it is a place for developing an independent and consistent self-identity based on a morality that allows the learner to ask *why* about the how's and when's that the culture demands

(2) The methods used by many teachers—and by the system of education itself—to address the issues of how and when represent activities more properly described by the use of the terms, *instruction* and *training,* as contrasted to *teaching* and *education,* which historically have been used to describe activities for seeking answers to the issues of why in behavior.

(3) Our often random use of the terms instruction, teaching, training, and education lead to a conceptual confusion about the process of learning that is compounded by the many constituencies that influence teaching and schooling—constituencies that have their own meanings for these terms.

(4) The historical influence of a dominant theory of learning, which emphasizes the primacy of performance as a definition of learning, has supported an instruction and training solution to learning tasks in schools. The Law of Effect, invented by E. L. Thorndike, represents a principal ingredient in this influence. The development of an evaluation and measurement orthodoxy that depends upon the testing of short-term learning represents a second, and interdependent, influence on the prevalence of an instruction-training solution to the objectives of teaching.

(5) The ability of schools and teachers to deal with the issues of good or bad, right or wrong, should or ought, and why, in their dedication to shaping and changing behavior is

impeded by definitions of learning that emphasize the improvement of measurable performance resulting from short-term instruction for the improvement of techno-behaviors. A commitment to a morality of education should lead to long-term inquiry about the phenomenon of self and the meaning that the process of experience has in shaping an identity based on commitments to a logic of ethics, rather than on a logic of skills.

(6) The examination of such issues as morality, the good life, and self-identity are not encouraged by a system of education that de-emphasizes a concern for the *process* of learning. To value the products of learning, that is, the performances or responses, to the exclusion of concern about the process that leads to any performance, is to reward only the answers and not the method by which they were derived. In many ways the process by which one arrives at an explicit behavior is more important than the behavior itself.

(7) If moral conduct is to be viewed as a desired outcome of our educational system, then we must examine the complex topology of teaching necessary to implement a moral commitment in education. The importance of any aspect of this topology for application to specific learning situations should not become an orthodoxy that denies the legitimacy of alternative aspects of the topology. Just as there are many faces to a culture, there are many faces to the way we teach to transmit that culture. To include ethics as part of the teachable aspects of a culture is to demand a view of teaching methods that matches teacher skills to learner needs. The teacher and the school exist to serve a multitude of purposes in our society. To allow any one of these purposes to force its methods on the school as a standardized solution to the issue of efficiency in learning is to rob schooling of the richness of experience that is possible when the questions of how, when, and why are all addressed in a logical and complimentary fashion, rather than in a competitive and mutually exclusive fashion. The reinforcing coexis-

tence in schools of many methods and purposes calls for the use of a rationale for teaching that is derived from what is effective in learning and not from what is efficient for learning.

(8) Two unfinished tasks in the discipline of education are the analysis and defintion of a morality of purpose for schooling, along with the transmission of a structure for the derivation of a moral order in the behavior of those who learn.

(9) The answers to the question of quality in the educational system of the United States are to be found in the impact that that system has on teaching the learner to seek solutions to curiosities about self and identity. To the degree that an educational system can provide a basis for helping the learner to solve in a productive manner the basic need for a human identity that is both individual and social, that system should be able to organize logically both the training and educational functions that must be met if schools are to promote a moral order. If this system of logic is to have any impact, it must address such issues as the appropriateness or inappropriateness of teaching method in relation to purpose, the value of behavior judged in terms of its impact on self and others, as well as the ethics involved in implementing evaluations for schooling based on the criteria of either efficiency or effectiveness as values for controlling and predicting the impact of schooling on the learner.

To have a moral education is not only to be guided toward the internalization of a system of ethics; it is also to benefit from a process that is itself guided by a morality that is inclusive yet empirical, capable of being analyzed but always demanding further analysis, and based on the assumption that the major function of any educational process is to expand the learner's awareness of himself. Let us examine in more detail some of the observations presented above to see how they might relate to the inclusion of a commitment to morality in education.

Training and Education

No one would deny that the total effort of formal school-ing, from kindergarten onwards, should legitimately include experiences that are both training and educational in their functions. One must have skills that result from effective in-struction in order to profit from teaching that encourages self-discovery. One major dilemma of our system of mass education is its inability to articulate logical conceptual models for its training functions as opposed to its educational functions. Any examination of the literature about schooling emphasizes the lack of meaningful differences in the common use of the terms training and education. Certainly we have issues that call attention to these differences. The debate concerning the relative merits of the liberal arts versus voca-tional training in higher education represents one set of issues that are frequently discussed by using the designations of in-struction, training, teaching, and education interchangeably as if they meant the same constellation of operations. Crawford has contributed a useful distinction between these concepts in his discussion of the role of training in the development of a system.[2] He describes the differences between training and education as follows:

(1) Training activities are those that are linked to the needs of a specific system; for example, we train physicians to meet the demands of the system of health care we have in this country.

(2) A definite program of instruction accompanies the training activities. The purpose of this program of instruc-tion is to prepare the learner to *perform* specific jobs within the system for which the training efforts are designed.

(3) The evaluation of training efforts is done by deter-mining the extent to which training contributes to the ob-jectives of the system it serves.

(4) Education attempts to prepare the learner for en-counters with the *many* systems that make up a society.

(5) Programs that are educational in nature are not "job bound." Teaching activities to meet educational needs are directed more toward the intrinsic needs of the learner rather than the extrinsic needs of particular systems.

(6) The value of education is assessed in terms of its impact on the growth and development of the individual, and not in terms of the contribution made to a specific system.

Training has a specific connotation of treating or manipulating a learner so as to bring him to some goal. Education, on the other hand, indicates a leading of the learner, usually in the direction of the development of a personal maturity as a function of the amount of education received. Historically, teaching and the teacher have been associated with the process of education, while instruction and the instructor have been associated with the tasks of training. One does not need to read far in the literature about teaching to find that these terms are not used with any sense of the potency of meaning that they should have if teaching is to be based on a system of defensible ethics.

The distinction between teaching and instruction is discussed by Green in his analysis of the many facets of teaching.[3] He points out that teaching and training are not identical, and says that "training is only a part of teaching. There are contexts in which it would be a rank distortion to substitute the one concept for the other."[4] Only in one important respect does training have a position of importance in those activities described as teaching. Green indicates this link in the following quotation from his discussion:

> . . . training resembles teaching insofar as it is aimed at actions which display intelligence. In this respect, training has a position of central importance in the coterie of activities we include in teaching. Ordinarily, however, the kind of inteligence aimed at in training is limited. What it excludes is the process of asking questions, weighing evidence, and, in short, demanding and receiving a justification of rules, principles, or claims of fact.[5]

Without the linkage stipulated above, the concept of training becomes a form of conditioning. Green also comments on the relationship between teaching and instruction at another point in his article:

> . . . teaching and giving instruction are not the same thing . . . whenever we are involved in giving instruction, it follows that we are engaged in teaching; but it is not true that whenever we are engaged in teaching, we are giving instruction.[6]

Teaching, then, represents a higher order of conceptualization of the activities that make education a meaningful and personal interaction between the teacher and the learner. To keep this process only at the level of instruction and training is to deny both the teacher and the learner access to the modes of inquiry that are demanded if education is to meet the needs of the learner rather than the demands of the discrete systems in our society.

Another way to look at the differences between instruction and teaching would be to examine the kinds of educational objectives that Bloom and his associates have established as necessary for a logic of learning to be in command of the teaching act.[7] Implicit in the Bloom taxonomy is a hierarchy of learnings that represents the full spectrum of objectives for education. The process of teaching should encompass this range if it is to be based on any consistent system of ethics to guide the behavior of the teacher. This hierarchy can be described as follows:

(1) *Acquiring knowledge.* Learning appropriate units of information and being able to recall what has been retained.

(2) *Comprehending what one has learned.* Developing the ability to understand what is being communicated and make use of the idea in some discrete way. This ability requires knowledge.

(3) *Learning to apply what one knows and comprehends.* This involves the ability to use principles and theories in concrete situations, and it requires success in acquiring knowledge and comprehending what is known.

(4) *Developing the ability to analyze what has been learned.* In order to analyze effectively, the learner must be able to break down information into logical parts and to understand the organization of ideas. Analysis requires application skills, the ability to comprehend, and knowledge.

(5) *Learning to synthesize what one knows.* This involves the ability to reorder parts and elements from previous learnings so that they are reformulated into a whole that reflects the perceptions of the learner as much as the demands of reality. Learning to synthesize effectively is to learn to avoid solipsism and at the same time to reaffirm a sense of self through the synthesis that emerges. Learning to synthesize is built upon the preceding four levels of learning.

(6) The most complex learning task for education is the *development of the ability to value.* Valuation involves learning to judge, according to some consistent criteria, the worth (value) of ideas, activities, and other behaviors. Learning to value in a manner that rewards a sense of personal worth involves knowledge, the ability to comprehend, apply, analyze, and a synthesis of these into some personal schema or model of self.

Most of what passes for teaching at all levels of education is directed toward meeting the demands of the first four elements in the hierarchy. The methods involved in attaining these objectives fit more readily into an instruction and training philosophy, particularly with respect to gaining knowledge, learning to comprehend communication, and developing the ability to apply what has been learned. Educational reform generally is directed toward finding ways to expand the process of education to include a demonstrated concern for, and an attempt to impact, the ability to

synthesize and to value in students. In fact, one could place
the terms training and instruction adjacent to the first element in the hierarchy, and education and teaching adjacent
to the last one, and from this parallelism see how training and
educational functions are distributed for the teacher, depending on the particular objectives that teaching addresses.

The inability of the teacher to articulate a logic that
clearly identifies the training and educational objectives in
teaching has many causes. These range from the constraints
in teacher-preparation programs to the inability of individual
teachers to go beyond the level of applying what they have
learned about teaching. In most instances, the preparation of
teachers is aptly described by the label "teacher training."
One dominant influence that has contributed to our confusion about teaching has been the directions that philosophies
of education have taken towards defining education as a
humanistic encounter, with the dominant learning theory for
education remaining essentially a behaviorism cut from the
cloth of E. L. Thorndike and his Law of Effect.

The Primacy of Performance in Learning

The point of view about learning offered by E. L.
Thorndike during the period between 1898 and the 1930s, is
now felt through the behavioristic approach made popular by
B. F. Skinner,[8] who represents a logical extention of the Law
of Effect proposed by Thorndike in 1898. This basic law of
learning emphasizes the importance of the effect of a response
that a learner makes on the strength of the bond between
that response and the stimulus that initiated it. Thorndike
called attention to the central role of a response, an overt behavior, a performance, in strengthening this connection. The
effectiveness of learning was to be judged on the strength of
the connection, and could be measured in a number of ways,
usually through testing retention of the ability to recall what
had to be learned. The contemporary version of this connec-
tionism, which Skinner has advanced through its method of

application known as the behavior modification theory, calls attention also to the centrality of performance and overt behavior.

The evolution of measurement and evaluation in schools followed the lead offered by Thorndike. The testing industry is devoted to collecting, quantifying, and evaluating the performance of students at all levels. The material that teachers have at their disposal to unfold the order of the curriculm is designed to provide incremental learnings that are, for the most part, assessed through the evaluation of responses learners make to achievement tests, diagnostic tests, competency tests, and other kinds of instruments, all of which are designed to compare performance and quantify effort.

All of this is not to deny the importance of a performance in learning. However, when teaching becomes an activity that is evaluated on the basis of how efficiently a teacher can change the short-term behaviors of students, then the art of teaching has given way to the science of instruction, and much of the richness and long-range impact of teaching is downgraded to a level of lesser importance for the time allocated to teaching. Yet contrasting points of view about learning have much to offer teachers if the supporters of our schools would allow them to begin to ask questions about education that have often been avoided in the past.[9] Humanistic approaches to teaching and learning offer promise for breaking out of the orthodoxy of behaviorism and its hold on teaching and learning. Much is being written about values education for students, but, as Hodgkinson points out,[10] very little if anything is being done to introduce values education into the programs of teacher preparation so that the teacher's values become the central concern before he becomes involved in values education with students. The behavioristic model for learning supports a system of ethics that is enriched by training models for instruction. Its emphasis on the overt response and the reinforcing effects of something pleasant that may accrue as a result of the response gives this point of view a mechanistic and physical extrinsic thrust. Training is indigenous to such a philosophy. In discussing the role of schools in moral development, Trow indicates three areas in which education can have an impact on the such development of students. [11] These are:

(1) The influence of the curriculum.
(2) The influence of how the teacher teaches.
(3) The influence of the teacher as reflected in the person who teaches.

We will see in last section of this chapter that the models that teachers have for human nature can influence the styles of teaching. Successful teaching if it is to be built on a sustaining system of ethics, must involve a moral commitment on the part of the teacher that seeks to find ways to teach that are appropriate to the individuality of the learner as well as to the particular hierarchy of objectives being employed. The system of ethics is not linear, that is, it is not unyielding over time. The moral development of the teacher throughout a career will include much revision and reordering of ethical considerations, but always with the aim of advancing the maturity and development of the learner toward more independent and insightful confrontations with reality.

Ethics and Teaching

The consideration of ethics as an integral aspect of teaching focuses attention on a conceptualization of the dual processes of teaching and learning in relationship to the self. Most teachers, particularly those in high schools and in higher education, are conditioned almost exclusively by their academic disciplines. We like to feel that the various disciplines are controlled by the knowledge scholars create for them. Realistically, the reverse may be the case. The teacher may not always be the master; in many ways, to attain any degree of recognition as an expert in any field, one must accept the subtle imprint of that discipline's logic and behavioral directives. Try as we may to escape such controls, we find ourselves judging a colleague's thinking in terms of the view of reality that we learned in our own academic study as the "correct" one.

Where moral influence is concerned, it is useful to think about teaching and learning as an expression *of* self rather than an abstraction *from* self. Such an approach can be incorporated in a model with three major themes.[12] The first concerns the patterns, or perceptions, everyone holds for human nature. Whether we talk about such impressions in more abstract terms such as a definition of the nature of the person, or whether we deal with them as simple conversations about the question, "Who am I?," these patterns still relate to notions we have about purpose, self-image, and the I-Thou interactions that provide a sense of personal identity.

A second theme places an accent on teaching and learning, and emphasizes the indeterminate and complex nature of goodness in teaching. Teaching is not an activity for which one can develop formulas to be applied with equal effects to all. Nor is it a process that can be described, in toto, as either art or science; more realistically, it is a subtle blending of the creative and the objective. There are many ways to teach successfully, and one person's success can be another's failure, even when conditions are identical. In short, effective teaching—the good or bad influence of the process—is a complexity of processes and relationships that are only now being appreciated.

The development of faculty members as human beings over time is a third theme of this model. Not much is known about adult human development. However, we do know that the beliefs, values, and attitudes that we have at one point in our lives may subsequently change. If there is any universal psychological truth about the human organism, it is the certainty of change in the way we view ourselves and others as we grow older and mature.

Any analysis of teaching and learning as expressions of the self must be viewed as a task that recognizes that what may be important to a person at one time in life may have

lesser importance at another time. What we do as teachers to
reinforce our feelings of importance about ourselves at one
stage of our careers may not be what we should do at another
time. The dimensions of change in our teaching that relate to
the order of our own human development are conditioned by
the basic concepts we have of self and the identity that give
meaning to our whole existence.

Allport, whose thinking supports the first, or human
nature, component of this model, identified three main-
streams of thinking about human nature in relationship to
the kinds of approaches psychology has taken to understanding human behavior. He observed:

> However excellent one's natural eyesight may be, a
> (teacher) always looks at a student through professional
> spectacles. It could not be otherwise. After all, the
> (teacher) has invested time and money in training. Of
> what use is it unless it adds special prisms to one's own
> unaided eyesight? The lenses we wear are ground to the
> prescription of our textbooks and our teachers. Even
> while we are undergraduates a certain image of the nature
> of (the person) is fitted to our eyes. We grow accus-
> tomed to the images and when we become practitioners
> or (teachers) we may still take it for granted. But every
> so often comes a time for optional reexamination. Perhaps
> the image we have is still the best fit we can get, perhaps
> it is not. We can tell only by examining alternative
> lenses.[13]

The three images Allport suggests as worthy of scrutiny
are:

(1) *The person seen as a reactive being.* The labels typi-
cally given to this image include: naturalism, positivism, behaviorism, operationalism, and physicalism. This point of
view holds human beings to be no different in kind from any
other living beings. Therefore, like the paramecium or the
pigeon people may be studied biologically, behaviorally, or

mathematically. According to Allport, if we ask, "What does it mean to be a human being?" this school of thought replies, "Man is one more creature of nature, his behavior, though complex, is predictable in principle. His present state is determined by his past state. A man's consciousness is unreliable and must be distrusted, perferably disregarded altogether. We seek the general laws of nature, not personal uniqueness. We study man, not men; objective reality, not subjective." [14]

In our present technological age, Allport's first rubric describes the mechanical person. Such an individual, in many ways, is a passive recipient of the stimuli around him, and reacts to such stimuli by initiating more. An almost mechanistic hedonism rules here, and the individual is often lost in the faceless organism called a species. Such terms as stimulus and response, input-output, behavior modification, shaping, and other catch words of our present technological society emerge from this conceptualization. The processes of "telling" and "testing," as teaching techniques, have much kinship with this point of view about human nature.

(2) *The person seen as a reactive being in depth.* This image is found in much that surrounds us in the marketplace, in our literature, and on television. The mechanical nature of the person has not changed. What has been added is a background of Freudian depth that, in its present-day manifestations, Freud himself might have difficulty recognizing. Here we have the dimensions of the unconscious, repression, regression, resistance, implicit motivation, and latent sexuality that influence many of the forms of our cultural expression today. The Freudian impact on education, especially on teaching and learning, has been great. A concern for feelings as well as reaction in learning has its origin to a great extent in the Freudian revolution. The major contribution that Freud made to our understanding of human nature is the emphasis on the past history of an individual as a shaping influ-

ence on the present. The past can easily become an excuse for inaction in teaching as well as a rationalization for the reactions we observe in our students. An emphasis on the past as the shaper of the future can often lead to a disregard for the potential that any person has to shape his own future. As teachers, it is very easy for us to rationalize our own inadequacies by blaming them on what students bring to us. Education is often viewed as a process for confronting the past, but it should go far beyond that. To be effective, education must lead to a transformation of what is recovered. The challenge for viewing human nature in terms of the depth that is behind our reactions is the challenge of using this knowledge of human capacity for the purpose of obtaining a revised sense of personhood.

This leads to the third point of view, which Allport labels:

(3) *The person seen as a being-in-process-of-becoming.* The phrase "being-in-process-of-becoming" represents a unified concept that indicates the existential commitment that can grow out of the other two points of view. Many people have difficulty understanding what is meant by the "process of becoming" simply because their own educational experiences have not prepared them to rediscover and to re-create their own identity. Allport explains what he means by the statement:

From the existential point-of-view, the ideal (teacher) will strive to develop two attitudes in (students). Taken separately they seem antithetical; but fused into a world view they provide strength for the furture. One attitude is tentativeness of outlook. Since certainties are no longer certain, let all dogmas be fearlessly examined, especially those cultural idols that engender a false sense of security; dogmas of race supremacy, of naive scientism, of unilinear evolutionary process. Let one face the worst in one's self and the world around us, so that one may correctly estimate the hazards. Taken by itself, such tentativeness, such insightfulness, might well lead to ontological despair. An acceptance of the worst does not prevent us from making the best of the worst. Humans have a remarkable ability to blend a tentative outlook with firm commitment to chosen values.[15]

The second attitude is that of *commitment*, which emerges from the tentativeness necessary to examine our existence and to produce a commitment. A commitment, in a sense, is a wager. One may lose it, but one may also win. The ability to commit grows out of a sensitive and insightful examination of our personal existence, which is not bound by an artificial chronology; it is continuous and multi-dimensional in what it brings to our ability to make personal commitments about self. It is not based upon the past alone nor does it imply action and performance as evidence of existence.

What Broudy has to say about teaching relates directly to Allport's concepts.[16] He identifies three prescriptions for the improvement of teaching: didactics, heuristics, and philetics. Didactics refers to those processes that involve the imparting and reinforcing of skills and knowledge, the things teachers do in the classroom. Included are those forms of learning that can be made explicit and evaluated as performance on the part of the student. According to Broudy, didactics depend heavily on extrinsic motivation. When knowledge is organized for didactics, it is in a logical and a necessarily psychological order.

The heuristic approach aims to manage teaching so that the student thinks for himself. Such thinking can be directed toward discovery of a solution to a problem, the achievement of insight into a situation, or the development of an induction in some field. Creativity in learning is often associated with this approach. A classic example of heuristical teaching was supplied by Socrates. Socratic thinking was the orginal model for discovery learning. John Dewey extended this approach into his analysis of problem solving. According to

Broudy, [17] heuristical teaching solves the problem of relevance by beginning with the learner's predicaments. One can clearly see the relationship between didactics and heuristics, particularly with respect to the prior scholastic accomplishments of the students.

The third type of teaching is philetics. The term is derived from the Greek word philos, which means loving. This prescription suggests that the secret of successful teaching is love, that is, the love of the teacher by the learner and vice-versa. Concern for the student's development, both intellectually and as a person, is the criterion in philetics. According to Broudy, given this philetic relationship, it is held that motivation and mastery will take care of themselves. This is explained by the theory that the love relationship removes the psychological blocks to learning, such as insecurity, fear of failure, fear of rejection, alienation from peers and parents, and numerous other emotional ills that inhibit learning.

The relationship of ethics to teaching and the extent to which teachers can influence the moral development of students is determined by the teaching-learning relationships teachers have with their students. These bear on certain notions about human nature. The successes and failure that we as teachers achieve in matching style with the concept of self should inevitably lead to continual reevaluation of style and self. One may choose a didactic approach as the most comfortable style at one point in a career, perhaps an early stage, because it has relevance to a self-image as a reactive being. Yet fixation on this single approach is likely to leave professional satisfactions unfulfilled because of its limited ethical and moral impact on students. Essentially, the ethics of teaching prescribe the search (by the teacher) for a satisfactory expression of self and the constant rediscovery of new dimensions of self.

The decision to train or to educate is a moral one. The choice has consequences for learners, the society as well as the individual teacher. Thus, the pursuit of professional effectiveness and moral accountability in teaching is highly personal, many times private, and intensely sensitive to the kinds of insights that analysis of beliefs and experience offers. Ethical impact in teaching may not come so much from outward activity; it may evolve from quiet contemplation about goals, relationships, and long-term outcomes. Listening to teaching may be as important as teaching itself if one is to develop the personal flexibility necessary to participate with any sense of deep and lasting satifaction in the teaching-learning process. Neither teaching nor learning can have lasting significance unless it takes its direction from the basic cross-cultural ethical and moral tenets that support civilized human existence. One's self-image as a teacher, at any stage in a career, and regardless of the methods employed, is, therefore, derived from an understanding of and a commitment to a personal moral value structure that is compatible with the survival needs of the social system.

[1]Patricia K. Cross, *Accent on Learning* (San Francisco: Jossey-Bass, 1976), pp. 3—23.

[2]M. P. Crawford, "Concepts of Training," in *Psychological Principles in Systems Development*, ed. R. Gagne (New York: Holt, Rinehart & Winston, 1965), pp. 301—42.

[3]Thomas F. Green, "The Topology of the Teaching Concept," *Studies in Philosophy and Education* 3 (Winter, 1964—65): 284—319.

[4]Ibid., p. 286.

[5]Ibid., p. 287.

[6]Ibid., p. 288.

[7]B. S. Bloom, ed., *Taxonomy of Educational Objectives: The Classification of Educational Goals.* Handbook I, Cognitive Domain, (New York: McKay, 1956).

[8]E. R. Hilgard, and G. H. Bower, *Theories of Learning* 4th ed. (Englewood Cliffs, N. J.: Prentice-Hall, 1975), pp. 28—61, 206—51.

[9]B. Claude Mathis, and William C. McGaghie, "From Theories for Learning to Theories for Teaching," in *Theories for Teaching*, ed. Lindley J. Stiles (New York: Dodd, Mead, 1974), pp. 30—50.

[10]C. Hodgkinson, "Values Education at One Remove," *Phi Delta Kappan* 58: 3 (November, 1976): 269—71.

[11]M. Trow, "Higher Education and Moral Development," *AAUP Bulletin* 62: 1 (1976): 20—27.

[12]Gordon W. Allport, "Psychological Models for Guidance," *Harvard Educational Review* 32: 4 (1962): 373—81.

[13]Ibid., p. 373.

[14]Ibid., p. 374.

[15]Ibid., p. 378.

[16]Harry S. Broudy, "Didactics, Heuristics, and Philetics," *Educational Theory* 22 (1972): 251—61.

[17]Ibid., p. 252.

Bibliography

Aiken, H. D. *Reason and Conduct.* New York: Alfred A. Knopf, 1962.

Allport, Gordon W. "Psychological Models for Guidance," *Harvard Educational Review* 32 (1962).

Anthony, James. "The Reaction of Adults to Adolescents and Their Behavior," *Adolescence: Psychosocial Perspectives.* Edited by G. Caplan and S. Lebovici. New York: Basic Books, 1969.

Arbuckle, Donald S. *Guidance and Counseling in the Classroom.* Boston: Allyn & Bacon, 1957.

————. *Teacher Counseling.* Cambridge, Mass.: Addison-Wesley Publishing Co., Inc., 1950.

Baier, Kurt, and Rescher, Nicholas. *Values and the Future.* New York: The Free Press, 1971.

Berne, Eric. *Games People Play.* New York: Castle Books, 1964.

————. *Principles of Group Treatment.* New York: Grove Press, 1966.

————. *Transactional Analysis in Psychotherapy.* New York: Castle Books, 1961.

Bettleheim, Bruno. "Moral Education," *Moral Education/Five Lectures.* Edited by Nancy F. Sizer and Theodore R. Sizer. Cambridge, Mass.: Harvard University Press, 1970.

Boston Schoolmaters. *Remarks on the Seventh Annual Report of the Honorable Horace Mann, Secretary of the Massachusetts Board of Education.* Boston, 1844.

Briggs, Jean L. *Never in Anger: Portrait of an Eskimo Family.* Cambridge, Mass.: Harvard University Press, 1970.

Broudy, Harry S. "Didactics, Heuristics, and Philetics," *Educational Theory, 22 (1972).*

Brown, Roger. *Social Psychology.* New York: The Free Press, 1965.

Brubaker, Dale L. *The Teacher as a Decision-Maker.* Dubuque, Iowa: William C. Brown Company, 1970.

Campbell, Donald T. "On the Conflicts Between Biological and Social Evolution and Between Psychology and Moral Tradition." *American Psychologist,* 30 (1975).

Century III Foundation. *Discover a Common Sense Moral Standard via Value Analysis.* Oak Brook, Ill.: The Foundation, 1976.

Church, Robert L. and Sedlak, Michael W. *Education in the United States: An Interpretive History.* New York: The Free Press, 1976.

Commager, Henry Steele, ed. *McGuffey's Fifth Eclectic Reader.* New York: The New American Library, 1962.

Crawford, M. P. "Concepts of Training," *Psychological Principles in Systems Development.* Edited by R. Gagne. New York: Holt, Rinehart & Winston, 1965.

Cremin, Lawrence A. *American Education: The Colonial Experience, 1607-1783.* New York: Harper & Row, 1970.

Cremin, Lawrence A. *The Transformation of the Schools: Progressivism in American Education, 1876-1957.* New York: Alfred A. Knopf, 1961.

Cross, Patricia K. *Accent on Learning.* San Francisco: Jossey-Bass, 1976.

Deiser, R. Lincoln. *The Vice Lords*. New York: Holt, Rinehart & Winston, 1969.

Devereux, George. *From Anxiety to Method in the Behavioral Sciences*. New York: Moulton, 1967.

Dewey, John. *Moral Principles in Education*. Boston: Houghton-Mifflin Company, 1909.

———. *Theory of Valuation*. Chicago: The University of Chicago Press, 1939.

Dillman, Don H. and Christenson, James A. "Toward the Assessment of Public Values," *Psychological Abstracts* (1972).

Finkelstein, Barbara. "Pedagogy as Intrusion: Teaching Values in Popular Primary Schools in the Nineteeth Century," *History of Childhood Quarterly* 11 (1975).

Freud, Sigmund. *Civilization and Its Discontents*. Translated by James Strachey. New York: W. W. Norton & Company, 1962.

Fromm, Erich. *Escape from Freedom*. New York: Avon Books, 1966.

———. *Man for Himself: An Inquiry into the Psychology of Ethics*. Greenwich, Conn.: Fawcett, 1947.

Gans, Herbert J. *The Levittowners*. New York: Pantheon Books, 1967.

Ginott, Haim. *Between Teacher and Child*. New York: Macmillan Company, 1974.

Goble, Frank. *The Third Force*. Pasadena, Calif.: Thomas Jefferson Research Center, 1970.

Gordon, Ira. *The Teacher as a Guidance Worker*. New York: Harper Bros., 1956.

Green, Thomas F. "The Topology of the Teaching Concept," *Studies in Philosophy and Education* 3 (1964-65).

Hagen, Owen A. *Changing World/Changing Teachers*. Palisades, Calif.: Goodyear, 1973.

Harris, Thomas. *I'm OK—You're OK*. New York: Harper & Row, 1967.

Hilgard, E. R. and Bower, G. H. *Theories of Learning*. Englewood Cliffs, N. J.: Prentice-Hall, 1975.

Hodgkinson, C. "Values in Education at One Remove," *Phi Delta Kappan* 58 (1976).

Holt, John. *What Do I Do Monday?* New York: Dell Publishing Company, 1970.

James, M. and Jongeward, D. *Born to Win*. Reading, Mass.: Addison-Wesley, 1971.

Jersild, Arthur T. *When Teachers Face Themselves*. New York: Bureau of Publications, Teachers College, Columbia University, 1955.

Kaestle, Carl F. *The Evolution of an Urban School System: New York City, 1750-1850*. Cambridge, Mass.: Harvard University Press, 1973.

Kohlberg, Lawrence. "A Cognitive-Development Approach to Moral Education," *The Humanist* 32 (1972).

Krug, Edward. *The Shaping of the American High School, 1880-1920*. Madison, Wisc.: The University of Wisconsin Press, 1964.

Lannie, Vincent P. *Public Money and Parochial Education.* Cleveland, Ohio: Case Western Reserve University Press, 1968.

Lee, Gordon C., ed. *Thomas Jefferson on Education.* New York: Columbia University Press, 1961.

Lee, Patrick C. and Gropper, Nancy B. "Sex Role Culture and Educational Experience," *Harvard Educational Review* 44:3 (1974).

Lief, Harold L., M. D. "Anxiety Reaction," *Comprehensive Textbook of Psychiatry.* Edited by Alfred M. Freedman, M. D., and Harold I. Kaplan, M. D. Baltimore: Williams and Wilkins, 1976.

Lockwood, Alan L. "A Critical View of Values Clarification," *Teachers College Record* 77 (1975).

Lynd, Robert. *Knowledge for What?* Princeton, N. J.: Princeton University Press, 1939.

McDonald, Frederick J. *Educational Psychology.* 2nd ed. Belmont, Calif: Wadsworth, 1965.

Mann, Mary T. P. *The Life and Works of Horace Mann.* Boston, 1891.

Maslow, Abraham H. *New Knowledge in Human Values.* New York: Harper & Row, 1959.

——. *The Psychology of Science.* New York: Harper & Row, 1966.

Mathis, B. Claude and McGaghie, William C. "From Theories for Learning to Theories for Teaching." *Theories for Teaching.* Edited by Lindley J. Stiles. New York: Dodd, Mead, 1974.

Mills, C. Wright. *White Collar: The American Middle Classes.* New York: Columbia University Press, 1951.

Mirsky, Jeannette. "The Eskimo of Greenland," *Cooperation and Competition among Primitive Peoples.* Edited by Margaret Mead. Boston: Beacon Press, 1937.

Monod, Jacques. *Chance and Necessity.* New York: Alfred A. Knopf, 1971.

Moustakas, Clark. *The Authentic Teacher: Sensitivity and Awareness in the Classroom.* Cambridge, Mass.: Howard A. Doyle, 1966.

Mydal, Gunnar. "American Values and American Behavior: A Dilemma," *Democracy, Pluralism, and the Social Studies.* Edited by James P. Shaver and Harold Berlak. Boston: Houghton-Mifflin, 1968.

Perry, James F. and Smith, Phillip G. "Levels of Valuational Discourse in Education," *Theories of Value and Problems of Education.* Edited by Phillip G. Smith. Urbana, Ill.: The University of Illinois Press, 1970.

Piaget, Jean. *Six Psychological Studies.* Translated by Anita Tenzer. New York: Vantage Books, 1967.

Raths, Louis, et al. *Values and Teaching.* Columbus, Ohio: Charles E. Merrill Publishing Company, 1966.

Ravitch, Diane. *The Great School Wars: New York City, 1805-1973.* New York: Basic Books, 1974.

Redl, Fritz and Wineman, David. *Children Who Hate: The Disorganization and Breakdown of Behavior Controls.* New York: Macmillan Company, 1951.

Redl, Fritz. *When We Deal With Children: Selected Writings.* New York: The Free Press, 1966.

Reisman, David. *The Lonely Crowd.* New Haven, Conn.: Yale University Press, 1950.

Ringness, Thomas A. *The Affective Domain in Education.* Boston: Little, Brown and Company, 1975.

Rokeach, Milton. *The Nature of Human Values.* New York: The Free Press, 1973.

———. *The Open and Closed Mind.* New York: Basic Books, 1960.

Rudolph, Frederick, ed. *Essays on Education in the Early Republic.* Cambridge, Mass.: Harvard University Press, 1965.

Sarason, Seymour B., et al. *Psychology in Community Settings.* New York: John Wiley Sons, 1966.

Schultz, Stanley K. *The Culture Factory: Boston Public Schools, 1789-1860.* New York: Oxford University Press, 1973.

Simon, Sidney and Clark, Jay. *Beginning Values Clarification.* San Diego, Calif.: Pennant Press, 1975.

Simon, Sidney. *I Am Loveable and Capable.* Niles, Ill.: Argus Communications, 1975.

———. *Meeting Yourself Halfway.* Niles, Ill.: Argus Communications, 1974.

Simon, Sidney; Hawley, Robert C.; and Britton, David. *Composition for Personal Growth.* New York: Hart Publishing Company, 1973.

Simon, Sidney; Howe, Leland W.; and Kirschenbaum, Howard. *Values Clarification.* New York: Hart Publishing Company, 1972.

Smith, B. Orthanel; Cohen, Saul B.; and Pearl, Arthur. *Teachers for the Real World.* Washington, D. C.: American Association of Colleges for Teacher Education, 1969.

Steiner, Claude M. *Scripts People Live.* New York: Grove Press, 1974.

Stewart, John. "Clarifying Values Clarification," *Phi Delta Kappan* 51:10 (1975).

———. *Toward a Theory for Values Development Education.* Lansing, Mich.: Michigan State University Press, 1974.

Strang, Ruth. *The Role of the Teacher in Personnel Work.* New York: Bureau of Publications, Teachers College, Columbia University, 1953.

Superka, D. "Approaches to Values Education," *Social Science Education Newsletter* 21 (1974).

Trow, M. "Higher Education and Moral Development," *AAUP Bulletin* 62:1 (1976).

Vassar, Rena, ed. *Social History of American Education.* Chicago: Rand McNally, 1965.

Weber, Max. *Gesammelte Aufsatze zur Soziologie und Sozialpolitik.* Tübingen: J. C. B. Mohr, 1924.

Yankelovich, Daniel. *The New Morality.* New York: McGraw-Hill Book Company, 1974.

Index

254

142 8 556